\# Felon With F

MY ADDICTION & RECOVERY

\# Big Felon

*Just Because You're Done with Drugs,
Doesn't Mean Drugs Are Done with You*

Book on amazon
↓
Reform and Rehabilitation for Virginia
↓
Learn to get your gun Rights as a felon

ED KRESSY

Today

Copyright © 2020 by Ed Kressy

All rights reserved. No part of this publication may be reproduced, distributed, or transmitted in any form or by any means, including photocopying, recording, digital scanning, or other electronic or mechanical methods, without the prior written permission of the publisher, except in the case of brief quotations embodied in critical reviews and certain other noncommercial uses permitted by copyright law.

ISBN: 978-1-95-036716-0

Published by

If you are interested in publishing through Lifestyle Entrepreneurs Press, write to: *Publishing@LifestyleEntrepreneursPress.com*

Publications or foreign rights acquisition of our catalog books. Learn More: *www.LifestyleEntrepreneursPress.com*

Printed in the USA

Certain names, locations, and identifying characteristics are changed. Some characters are composites. Dialogue and events are recreated from memory and, in some cases, compressed to convey the substance of what was said or what occurred.

Ten percent of the author's profits are donated to Defy Ventures, a nonprofit delivering training in entrepreneurism and employment to currently and formerly incarcerated men and women.

Dedicated to all of you who have ever entered the doors of the Henry Ohlhoff House, San Francisco… whether in the flesh, or in spirit.

When you get into a tight place and everything goes against you, till it seems as though you could not hold on a minute longer, never give up then, for that is just the place and time that the tide will turn.

—Harriet Beecher Stowe

Contents

Introduction: Reggie 1
One: Sentences 7
Two: The Cellar Hole 14
Three: Weddings 22
Four: Lies 34
Five: Poem 45
Six: Bangkok 54
Seven: Home on Monterey Boulevard 65
Eight: Mickey 76
Nine: The Boolean Operators 87
Nine-and-a-Half: Theories 100
Ten: The FBI 110
Eleven: Imprisonment & Freedom 121
Twelve: Haikus 129
Thirteen: The Interview 146
Fourteen: Sebastian 165
Fifteen: Campaigns 185
Sixteen: Tigers' Cave 207
Seventeen: Krav Maga 228
Eighteen: Awards 236
Nineteen: Families 268
Twenty: Hands 275

Introduction: Reggie

What we dwell upon is who we become.

—Oprah Winfrey

Meet a man we'll call Reggie. You may already know him, or know of him…

You may have seen him lurking in doorways or shambling along sidewalks of your city or town.

Reggie's been addicted to drugs for over half his life.

For the past eleven years, he's been addicted to methamphetamine.

For the past four-and-a-half years, he's been deep in meth psychosis.

He hasn't showered or brushed his teeth in months.

His face is scabbed from picking at worms he felt tunneling under his skin.

He wears the same clothes every day: A grimy black baseball jacket, filthy Ben Davis slacks, Converse sneakers held together with duct tape. No socks; no underwear.

At night he wears a tuxedo he "cleans" with shoe polish.

In his mind, a vast FBI conspiracy targets him.

The FBI communicates with him using hypnosis, subliminal messaging, top-secret technology.

One minute, the Bureau is out to frame him because he

knows about a high-level government coverup.

Plans to send him to prison for life, assassinate him, or have him kidnapped and tortured to death.

The next minute, he's a top-secret undercover FBI operative. The Bureau recruited him, trained him, delivers him telepathic instructions.

As he goes about his FBI business, he mutters curses and screams at people who aren't even there. The disembodied voices he hears are such a big part of his life—and have been for so long—he's given them a name.

He calls them the "Boolean Operators."

Reggie is sure the Boolean Operators are connected to the FBI. He just can't figure what he's supposed to do about it.

The Boolean Operators heckle, threaten, curse at, and talk about him, every waking minute. They are his worst enemies, and yet his only friends. He can't imagine life without the Boolean Operators. They are the cornerstone of his world, and his world is a universe away from the one in which most of us exist.

The Booleans' voices are indistinguishable from those of his family members and former friends. To Reggie, they might as well be the same. He believes those family members and former friends watch and listen to him always, through hidden cameras and microphones. Some of them implanted inside his body.

When he's hungry, Reggie steals from supermarkets, uses fraudulent food stamps, gobbles grub at the soup kitchens. Your tax dollars paid for his various incarcerations. The salaries of police officers, sheriff's deputies, FBI agents, and court officials who've had to deal with him.

Before the cops confiscated his .357 pistol, Reggie carried

Introduction: Reggie

it almost everywhere. As protection against the gangsters in the employ of rogue FBI agents he thought were after him. He's stolen from his family, vandalized countless properties, and mistreated the dog he once owned and loved more than anything.

What Reggie believes is real removes almost all hope of communicating his reality to others. It would just as difficult to convince Reggie the Boolean Operators and FBI conspiracies are delusions, just as it would be hard to convince you your dreams are real and your reality is a dream.

Reggie is scared to seek help. Afraid if he admits what's in his mind, he'll be committed to a psychiatric institution. Like he believes his family and former friends tried to do that one time, four years ago, under the guise of a drug intervention. So far as he's concerned, they'd do it again, if given the chance.

But he's not giving them the chance.

It isn't like Reggie never had opportunities. He owned a home but sold it and spent the money (along with his retirement accounts and life savings) on meth, strip clubs…guitars and electronics he smashed in fits of rage or tore apart looking for surveillance devices.

He turned his back on a promising career in biotechnology when it conflicted with his drug addiction.

And—it likely goes without saying—he is nowhere near employable.

How do you feel when you encounter Reggie?

Do you feel compassion, anger, fear, disgust, frustration?

Do you feel some mix of emotions…or something else entirely?

Are you not certain exactly how you feel?

Well…there's one more thing about Reggie you might want to know…

Reggie is me.

I am Reggie.

Or, rather, I *was* Reggie. Until autumn, 2007, when I finally put away the meth pipe for good.

Just because you're done with drugs, doesn't mean drugs are done with you. Years after getting clean, episodes of extreme FBI paranoia dogged me. To this day—over a decade drug-free—I still experience schizophrenic symptoms. My interpretation of the *Diagnostic and Statistical Manual of Mental Disorders* (the DSM is on its fifth edition; rumor has it will soon release a Greatest Hits album) is…I am schizophrenic. Nevertheless, I refer to myself as "experiencing schizophrenic symptoms" out of respect for persons handed a diagnosis, their loved ones, and caregivers.

I haven't had any sort of intimate relationship since quitting drugs.

I'm afraid to travel outside the United States…Mossad kidnappers, terrorist assassins.

My personal choice is not to use psychiatric medication…

Still, thanks to the amazing people I've encountered through the course of my recovery, I've gone from being Reggie—a drain on society's resources, a threat to his communities—to serving as a volunteer, and a resource for others facing similar obstacles as those I overcame. I've metamorphosed into a person who, like many others before me, proves transformation is possible.

I've been allowed to contribute to nonprofits, promote public safety, and appear before audiences at leading companies and educational institutions.

Incredibly, FBI Director Christopher Wray recognized me with his Director's Community Leadership Award. Thus I may be the only person who was once arrested by the FBI, and went on to receive a community service award from the director of the FBI.

This book intends to prove to you…

With the right help, those of us who overcome addiction are capable of giving to society.

I've been able to do it because remarkable people inspired me to live a spiritual life focused on helping others, overcoming fear, and achieving my dream.

My dream has always been to be a writer. I got closer in December 2016, when the website Vox published my article on my addiction. It generated positive response. Twelve hundred viewers "liked" it when popular San Francisco newscaster and good friend Frank Somerville posted it on his Facebook page. Frank's friends left comments:

"Thank you, Frank, for sharing this brave man's story. I work as a cardiac nurse and see far too many cases of meth addicts…it can be so hard on the heart."

"Thank you for your inspirational story! You never know who else might make a change by reading this."

"I hope this inspires addicts to find the strength for their own recoveries. Such an awesome turnaround."

Addicted persons and those who love them contact me out

of the blue to express appreciation. Sometimes, if they have questions or want someone to listen, we'll talk on the phone. Perhaps readers liked the article because of the intent behind it: to write about lessons I learned in a way that brings value to others. Thus, this book aims to give you a deeper understanding of addiction, by letting you inside the mind of an addicted person.

The dream gets closer....

Ultimately, with an addicted person like me, there's a disconnect between dreams and goals. To most, I would think, these things are similar, if not the same.

A dream is who we want to be; a goal is what we want to do.

A woman's dream is to be a business owner; her goal is to own a business. A man's dream is to be a marathoner; his goal is to run a marathon.

My dream of being a writer?

I never had the confidence, the faith, or belief in myself.

What could I possibly have that you might want to read about?

Instead I pursued goals.

Have a biotech career, own a home, compete in kickboxing.

Nothing wrong with any of them.

Yet for me those and other goals were superficial.

In a way, they held me prisoner.

I began the long process of setting myself free, by striving to achieve my dream. Ironically, I found some of the first stirrings of freedom in a most unlikely place…

Jail.

One:
Sentences

Let's say that he should go out and hang himself because he finds that writing well is impossibly difficult. Then he should be cut down without mercy and forced by his own self to write as well as he can for the rest of his life. At least he will have the story of the hanging to commence with.

—Ernest Hemingway (when asked what he would consider the best intellectual training for the would-be writer)

I follow Sheriff's Deputy Horne up the stairs to the visitor's area of San Bruno County Jail. It's Thanksgiving Day. San Bruno is the oldest operating county jail west of the Mississippi. Modeled after San Quentin Prison; used as a Japanese internment camp during World War Two. Dim corridors, crumbling cement, peeling paint. Tendrils of damp fog weave through rusted steel grilles covering windows without glass.

I'm serving a sixty-day sentence. San Francisco has devolved into a Draconian state...*it's illegal to walk around with a loaded .357 pistol in your waistband and a sixteenth of an ounce of meth in your pocket. What's next, no freedom of speech?*

"How's the kitchen shift going?" Deputy Horne is nonchalant, like one of my former colleagues at the Biotech Giant asking how a spreadsheet was shaping up. "I saw you mopping. What was there…a flood?"

"A bad pipe. I guess they found it."

Horne used to pitch for the San Francisco Giants. Another deputy brought in his baseball card once. We inmates crowded around to see it. When I first arrived in San Bruno, Horne took me aside. "There's a spot open on the kitchen shift," he said. "If I were incarcerated, I'd work. Start rebuilding my life."

It wasn't so much what he said as *how he said it*. Deputy Horne projected an image of a person *I wanted to be like*. His life had purpose. Of course, that purpose was to keep people like me in jail…still, Horne wanted to help people. Others in my life had purposes that worked for them. But not for me.

"Who's your visitor?" Horne asks. "Must care about you, to come to this godforsaken place on Thanksgiving." We've come to a locked door. Horne pushes a button on his walkie talkie, utters a few words of radio code.

"My uncle. I'm gonna show him my plan to get my life back together."

The door remains shut; Horne has to repeat his request. There's a metallic buzzing. As the door swings open, you see how thick it is. It reseals behind us with a heavy steel clang. There in the visitors' room, sitting by himself behind shatterproof glass, is my Uncle Jupiter. Wearing his silver and blue Rolex and a white tennis sweater.

You've seen TV shows with jailhouse visiting rooms? Inmates and visitors talking through telephones. Uncle Jupiter holds

One: Sentences

his in his fist.

"How're you doing, kiddo?"

Kiddo. I may be thirty-four, but Uncle Jupiter raised me almost as much as my biological dad. Going back to when I was sixteen and first came to California.

"I haven't punched anyone. Some guys deserve it." I'm trying to impress him by projecting a rugged side of myself. Jupiter grew up in the Bronx. Played point guard on the West Point basketball team. Fought in Vietnam. Served something like thirty years in the Army. At his retirement ceremony, he made a speech. Told a story about taking a knife from an enemy soldier in hand-to-hand combat. He wasn't bragging or anything. Years later, my self-defense instructors will teach me how hard it is to take a knife away from an attacker. In the movies it always looks easy.

"I've got a plan to get my life back together," I say.

A pause. Then, "That's good." Like he's considering a fact not supported by research.

"I'll show it to you."

"You'll *show it* to me?"

"Yes." I uncrumple a few scraps of notebook paper from the pocket of my orange jail suit. "I made a slideshow."

"A what?"

"A slideshow."

He's probably thinking the nephew's full around the bend...

"We don't have PowerPoint, of course." I unfold my crude drawings. I was never good at drawing. My grandfather was... he was an artist, even sketched Batman and the Lone Ranger in some of their first comic books. "The first thing I'm gonna do when I get out," I press the slide against the glass, "I've got some connections. Professional connections, that is," I'm quick to add. There's my scrawling of the headquarters of the Biotech Giant, the sprawling campus interwoven with a DNA strand that looks like a snake trying to swallow itself. "Then I'll re-connect with Logan." Logan is my old college roommate. I flip to the next slide. "Then what I'll do is get back into the gym—"

"Wait a minute," he says. "Slow down."

And now, it's okay.

I have Uncle Jupiter's attention.

I'm telling him what he wants to hear.

"What is that?" He points at a stick figure on one slide.

"It's me, training for kickboxing. See? There's the punching bag, the jump rope."

I could always get by with the small degrees of creativity, intellect, and humor the Universe blessed me with. Make jokes, get laughs, utilize my meager talents for writing. I'd hold my fears and doubts in check, to deal with later, alone—with my thoughts, with drugs.

"I'll be the best former jail inmate ever." Like most of the promises I make, I believe it.

"Okay, kiddo," Uncle Jupiter says. He tugs on his sleeve. The wool is fraying on the cuffs. Deputy Horne sits nearby; the olive green of his crisply pressed uniform set against the drab-white paint on the walls. Back to us; arms crossed. Like he's in the dugout, waiting for the inning to end.

"I gotta go," Jupiter says. "Thanksgiving dinner." He adjusts his fist around the telephone. "I called your parents. They're coming out when you get released."

I crumple the slides and stuff them into my pocket. "Thanks for letting me know."

I follow Deputy Horne to my home in the kitchen workers' dorm.

I'm sweeping the kitchen floors. Figure eights—*infinity loops*—with the broom. Detritus everywhere, from the frenzy of the breakfast shift. We've been at it since 2:00 a.m. Spooning reconstituted eggs onto food trays on the chow line, hauling sacks of oatmeal to cauldrons of boiling water, stirring grits into the industrial blender. The blender is four feet high. The other day, another inmate started to stick his hand into the spinning blades. The supervisor screamed, sprinting from the cutting board, yanking him away. He would've had a better chance of pulling his arm out of a jet turbine. The blender wouldn't have slowed down. His arm would've been served upstairs, mixed in with the grits.

I sweep and consider the future…

All the garbage about going back to work for the Biotech Giant. Why shouldn't Uncle Jupiter believe it? He donned uniforms of a West Point cadet and basketball player, the suit and tie of a city government official. Built status and financial stability, for himself and his family. You couldn't blame him for getting all fired up after me to do the same. And now I'd gone and told him I wanted to. In a slide presentation, no less.

"Hey," a voice calls. "Got a minute?" Deputy Horne strides up.

"What else do I have?" I grin, leaning on my broom.

Horne hands me a Styrofoam cup of steaming coffee. "Thanks for mopping the other day." The sheriff's star on his chest reflects the dull halogen bulbs. The coffee is real, from the deputies' off-duty room. Not the chicory they serve upstairs.

"I've been thinking," I say, "about what you said. Putting my life back together."

He looks up as if from the mound, tracing the path of a long fly ball. Headed towards the faraway foul pole…could be a strike, or a home run. A few inches either way determines whether he'll get sent to the dugout. "There's an opening on the Midnight Crew," he says. "Are you interested? Those guys eat like kings."

There's an odd sense of pride. The Midnight Crew is the most sought-after kitchen shift. Preparing food for the off-duty room. "Sounds like a promotion," I say.

"Let's go roll up your things," Horne says. "Just don't try going over the wall."

"No way. I'm gonna *tunnel*. Got my spoon."

Upstairs, I put my possessions on the thin blanket covering my foam-rubber mattress and roll it all into a tube. It's not much: toothbrush, razor, yellow legal pad, pens. I grip everything in a bear hug and follow Deputy Horne across the cement floor to where the guys working Midnight Crew sleep. In the kitchen dorm, inmates are grouped by work shift. In general population, they segregate themselves by race.

My yellow legal pad starts to slide, but Horne catches it, hands it back to me. I make up my bunk and take my pad to one of the steel tables that run along the center of the dorm. The tables are bolted to the floor and as solid as a submarine's hull.

I stare at the blank paper.

One: Sentences

The Boolean Operators' disembodied voices talk to me. Like they always do.

Just because you're done with drugs, doesn't mean drugs are done with you.

The Booleans assure me I'm an undercover FBI operative. Jail is part of my training.

My paranoia tells me the FBI conspiracy is afoot…I'll spend the rest of my life behind bars.

What could I possibly have that you might want to read about?

My mind circles, twists figure eights like the broom scraping the jailhouse kitchen floor. I think back to Bangkok—four years ago. Lacing up my running shoes, following Omar through the gates of the Muay Thai camp before the day's kickboxing training. Struggling to keep up with him as he makes the run through the tangled Bangkok streets.

I begin to write.

Two:
The Cellar Hole

...treasured among golden memories are the visions of matchless sublimity which delighted the childhood and youth of every absent son and daughter of Ashburnham.

—Ezra Stern, in his 1887 history of Ashburnham, Massachusetts

Two: The Cellar Hole

Ashburnham became incorporated in 1765. There's a "powder house" where Revolutionary War soldiers hid gunpowder from the British. Two thousand or so residents live in the town, my grandparents included. My grandfather, like I mentioned, was an artist. My grandmother wrote. She'd become friends with Lois Wilson, wife of Bill Wilson, co-founder of Alcoholics Anonymous, when they'd lived near each other in New York. It's believed my grandmother may even have lent some editorial help to the Wilsons as they drafted the original "Big Book" of Alcoholics Anonymous. The Big Book outlines the spiritual program of recovery followed by persons in AA.

My parents live near the New Hampshire border, atop a hill. For my younger sister, Blossom, and me, it means careening on sleds in winter; barreling after fireflies and garden snakes in summer. Beyond the kitchen picture window, all you see are trees, sky, and field. Maybe wild turkeys or deer, pecking, hunting for food.

And the vegetable gardens.

Dad grows vegetables when he's not teaching English at the local community college. He wrote a book, *How to Grow Your Own Vegetables*. The tomatoes require extra care. Dad starts them from seeds, mixing potting soil in plastic yogurt cups my mom saves. He sets them in the sun of the east-facing sheltered greenhouse. Spring trudges towards summer. Soon the fragile, foot-high seedlings are ready for transplant.

The outdoor garden west of the house can be harsh, fraught with danger. Blossom and I help wrap the stems in tinfoil, protection against underground cutworms. The stems are turgid, with a prickly fuzz. We twist loops of hairy twine around the stems and anchor them to stakes for support against gusting winds. We construct wire barricades to keep deer out. Dad does all he can to protect them; to get the vines to bear fruit. Often, that fruit is ripe and delicious.

My mom writes recipes and food articles for *The Boston Globe* and various periodicals. When the tomatoes ripen, she cuts them into wedges, which she sprinkles with sugar. I sit at the round wooden dining table off the screened-in porch, eating as fast as the wedges appear in front of me. Until one day I push it too far and vomit pinkish slime everywhere. It will be decades before I can even think about eating another raw tomato.

Blossom and I have an army of toy animals. Blossom is an amazing being…gentle, soulful, the spirit of an ancient poet in a tiny body topped with silken blonde hair. She and I assign names, elaborate backstories, unique personalities to our stuffed animals. "Slick," my favorite, is a muskrat our father made in his workshop from a triangular block of wood coated with gleaming shellac and a carefully twisted coil of copper for a tail. Slick rides a motorcycle and is a bit of a ne'er-do-well. Modeled after Fonzie from *Happy Days*, of course.

We stage musical plays for our parents, with toy animals as actors. Scoring our productions from record albums borrowed from the public library. If the librarian wonders why a ten year old and his kid sister keep checking out soundtracks to *West Side Story* and *Cabaret,* she doesn't ask. Blossom and I memorize the lyrics. After dinner, as the wood stove crackles and our home's ancient timbers creak, our parents laugh and clap as Slick the Muskrat and his merry band belt out their

words of wisdom:
When you're a Jet, you're a Jet all the way…
Life is a cabaret, old chum.

The Cellar Hole behind our house is an ancient foundation.

It's the place that's all mine.

Long before my birth, the Lane family settled down in what would become Ashburnham. They dug an earthen hole; reinforced it with stones dragged from the countryside. The house the Lanes built on that foundation has long since crumbled. My imagination begins to thrive.

I leap from stone to stone in the Cellar Hole. My mind creates fantasy characters; stages intergalactic battles with superhuman heroes and villains. Flying ships blast through space, passing beams through laser ports. Medieval armies lay siege

The Cellar Hole, where childhood dreams were born

to castles. Bands of heroes march against titans, dragons heave fire from scaly lungs. My mind invents a professional football league where players ride tall unicycles. Balancing, supporting one another with deft teamwork in the huddle. Smashing forth on their one-wheeled contraptions. Bursts of skill, grace, athleticism. Until the crunch of the tackle, and the men and cycles clatter to the turf. Only to right themselves and pedal back to the huddle. There are never any injuries, no lasting forms of trauma. Not in the Cellar Hole.

In junior high, I fantasize about things which prove almost as impossible as unicycle football. Playing on my school's Pop Warner team, for example. I'm soft, weak, uncoordinated. I make "taxi squad." I'm on the roster but don't suit up for games. I dream about starting a conversation with Natalie LaFontane, the girl at the locker next to mine. Sure, Natalie is pretty, but it isn't like I have romantic feelings for her. I just want to talk to a popular kid. Natalie is nice—not a snob or anything. But for me to choke out two words of conversation?

It never happens.

It doesn't help I have strange skin conditions and wear weird clothes. Am way too sensitive. Bus rides home from school, when the other kids get rowdy, the driver pulls over. Refusing to start the bus until everyone settles down. I cry on the bus… afraid I'll never get back to my Cellar Hole.

At Oakmont Regional High School (which included junior high), a kid best known for crying and being uncoordinated? Not a candidate for class president. I'm the last one picked for teams; the one who gets punched in the stomach in the locker room. The kids call me "Crusty" and knock my schoolbooks

Two: The Cellar Hole

and spiral notepads from my hands. I can't understand why the popular boys always talk about masturbation. They say it's only for losers, never do it themselves. Yet they sure seem to talk about it a lot.

I need a viable means of escape from the bullies and cliques of popular kids.

I find it in the Cellar Hole…

I find it in books.

Thanks to my father's teaching I learn to read early in life; he and my mother instill in me a love for books. To imagine my childhood home without books is like picturing it without a roof or floorboards. Leather-bound volumes with old-fashioned full-color plates depicting scenes from *Last of the Mohicans* or *Treasure Island*. Encyclopedia sets. Medical textbooks (my mom is a nursing instructor as well as a food writer). I bring home stacks of books from the library. C.S. Lewis, Judy Blume, S.E. Hinton. The *Hardy Boys* and J.R.R. Tolkien. The characters within those pages as alive as the bullfrogs and snakes Blossom and I catch and let go in the grass and ponds behind out home.

With books, when the world called *reality* isn't working (which it isn't, as I grow older), there's always somewhere else to go.

Writing becomes a way to create worlds I understand. Reading teaches me how words should appear on a page. I write a satire of Edgar Allan Poe's *The Cask of Amontillado*, titled *The Can of Coca-Cola*, about a boy defeating a bully in a haunted high-school hallway. I compose a story of a superhero, Aerosol Man. A giant half human/half spray can who overcomes enemies with jets of paint or cleaning fluid. He's blown up in the climax, returns to life in the denouement. I write a story about a man slipping into a coma. He's chased in his dreams by an ax-wielding specter wearing a motorcycle helmet with a tinted visor, as the heart monitor by his hospital bedside beeps its final signals.

My English teachers read my assignments to the class or call me to the front of the room to read them. Some of the few times I feel proud. High marks on tests or report cards don't matter. But knowing something I'd created *appeals to an audience*...there's a special feeling. The same bullies who punch me on the playground smile, clap me on the shoulder, tell me they like my story.

On my other school projects, I get "help" from my father. Meaning, since I'm too preoccupied with my fantasies to contribute much, those projects end up mostly his work. The pieces he produces in his basement workshop are museum-quality...Santa's elves couldn't rival their craftsmanship. A wood-block race car with a fire-engine red finish deeper than a Lamborghini's, a hand puppet of Galileo who could guest-star on the Muppet Show. An abacus made from Scrabble tiles that could power an early computer. I tote his creations to school, put my name on them, and get my "A".

But my writing is all mine. I invent the characters, the stories and scenes, and get them down on paper (Dad maybe proofreads).

I want to create something as beautiful as my dad creates... but I don't know how, at least with my hands. Yet my imagination gives birth to strange forms of beauty, and my hands can get what's in my imagination onto a page.

Two: The Cellar Hole

The teachers give *my father* an A on the race cars and hand puppets...
But those bullies like *my* stories.
Maybe I have something you might want to read about.
Writing becomes a form of sanctuary...
I'll soon find another sanctuary.
Drinking.

Three:
Weddings

...one glass of rum won't kill you, but if you take one you'll take another and another, and I stake my wig if you don't break off short, you'll die—do you understand that?—die, and go to your own place...the name of rum for you is death.

—Robert Louis Stevenson, *Treasure Island*

Summer, Brooklyn, 1984. Two weddings take place.

My aunt's nuptials at the Brooklyn Botanical Gardens...

And the marriage of my earliest feelings of social acceptance and being intoxicated.

Fourteen years old, drunk for the first time...the door to a new world about to open

Three: Weddings

There's a photograph from the reception held at my new uncle's apartment. A fourteen-year-old boy, necktie undone, stares down as he drinks from a glass of champagne.

I look up when I hear a voice off to my side.

"Yo, you the kid from Massachusetts? I guess we're cousins now." Jess is less than enthused. He's my age, but looking at him isn't like gazing into a mirror. Even at fourteen, here's a kid with *swagger*. He could be the Brooklyn-accented son of Don Johnson's character in *Miami Vice* (which will become my favorite show when it debuts a couple months later). Jess taps his champagne flute. "Wanna go downstairs and watch some porn?"

I shake my head, scared. Conditioned to freeze and act frightened (truth be told, it wasn't an act) when the bullies pick on me. Maybe they'll leave me alone. If I don't say anything to Natalie LaFontane, I won't say anything stupid.

"C'mon." Jess draws the word into seven or more syllables. *C'mahhhhhhhn...*

I shoot a nervous glance around. My parents laugh as Uncle Jupiter entertains them with a story. I want nothing more than to be Jupiter's best nephew. But my closest relatives may as well have touched down in flying saucers. Everyone else knows who they're supposed to be; what they're supposed to say.

"Okay," I tell Jess. "Let's do it." I follow him downstairs. His friend is set up with a VHS porno movie and two purloined bottles of champagne.

Even today, thirty-five years later, I remember a comment Jess's friend made, the plot of the movie (feel free to craft your own joke about plot lines and porno movies). I remember feeling part of something secret and forbidden. *I can get access.* The wedding guests, smiling at something I don't understand? Let them have their laughter.

You may have felt similar feelings when you chose a major in college, locked lips for your first kiss, or lost yourself in a book the author seemed to have written for you alone. For me, the bonds between the first stirrings of freedom and acceptance, and being intoxicated, will prove hard to break. Even psychosis and jail will not be enough. And, let's face it: Swilling champagne from the bottle while engrossed in porn is a lot easier than becoming a writer.

The following summer my parents take us to Heidelberg, Germany. Uncle Jupiter is stationed at the Army base. He picks us up at the airport in his Mercedes.

"This is the autobahn." Jupiter looks at me in the rearview mirror. "No speed limit." A few kilometers later, he spots a military vehicle and pulls alongside. He leans across my startled dad in the passenger seat, shouting at the soldier behind the wheel.

"Slow down! Your vehicle is traveling too fast!"

It confuses me. Uncle Jupiter feels there's a wrong to be righted. Rules broken by his subordinates. But why endanger lives with a shouting match on the no-speed-limit autobahn? He's wearing civilian clothes; no way for the other soldier, the one being yelled at, to know his rank.

That night Uncle Jupiter treats us to German spätzle, cordon bleu, and chocolate.

The next afternoon, we stroll through a town. Uncle Jupiter

Three: Weddings

taps me on the shoulder as we're stopped at a crosswalk. "Traffic signals are different here," he says, pointing. Sure enough, the "wait" sign is lit up with a silhouetted person with hands on hips and arms akimbo. Uncle Jupiter does a parody, smiling. I laugh and imitate his imitation.

We play tennis on clay courts the color of Mars' surface. Jupiter plays a champion-caliber game. I, unable to get the ball in play with an overhead serve, hurl my racquet into the net. That week, tennis star Boris Becker—born close by, in the town of Leimen—will become the youngest player ever to win Wimbledon. My own claim to fame will be less auspicious.

My older cousin Lynn and I sit on the living room floor, watching *The Road Warrior* on VHS. Lynn inherited Jupiter's athleticism, is a soccer standout. She dates a popular boy. Even were he not in the picture, Lynn wouldn't have to worry about a male suitor (or ten) making himself available.

"There's a festival tonight," she says. "My friends are going. Are you up for it?" Mel Gibson's character Mad Max careens over a sand dune, propels his souped-up car across a post-apocalyptic desert. Surrounded by incredible violence, taken in by a band of terrorized survivors who don't trust him but desperately need him just the same.

We take the streetcar to the festival. Lynn sits me down with her friends at a picnic table under a tent. Bands play; couples dance; festivalgoers smile and talk in a language I don't understand.

And German beer flows.

I don't just get drunk. I get *blackout drunk*. Not tipsy on champagne like at the Brooklyn wedding. Vomiting-in-the- bushes, staggering-home-with-Lynn-holding-me-upright drunk. We cross a moonlit lawn; a shape darts across my field of vision.

"Lynn!" I scream. "I'm hallucinating!"

Lynn's laughing.

"I thought a saw a rabbit!"

"There *are* rabbits," Lynn says, shifting as she supports my drunken weight. "They come out at night."

"I thought I was hallucinating," I mutter, kneeling. "Those rabbits are *real*." I vomit in the grass, stagger to my feet, and try to catch one sprinting across the lawn. It darts down a hole.

It's without question the greatest night of my life.

For many years I'll keep the *stein* I drank from. An enormous clay thing; more of a pot than a glass. What I remember most about that night isn't what it's like to be drunk. Or what the kids talked about at the picnic table (soccer and heavy metal, probably).

I never forgot the *feeling*. Surrounded by Lynn's friends… *these kids actually* like *me!* As local hero Boris Becker makes history at Wimbledon; there's a new type of success within my grasp. I can be part of a group; be like one of the popular kids.

The only difference between the kid sitting at the picnic table and the one spinning the combination to the locker next to Natalie LaFontane's?

Alcohol's been added to the mix.

Summer, San Francisco, 1986. Uncle Jupiter's been transferred to the Presidio of San Francisco, where he serves as Deputy Post Commander. I travel to California on my own (on my parents' dime, of course).

The Presidio: a military base of exquisite natural and human-created beauty. White buildings with red tile roofs sprinkled amongst lush greenery of lawns, palm fronds, eucalyptus forests. There's a Burger King with a picture window offering a sweeping view of the Golden Gate Bridge. I'm amazed the first time I see the Bridge…it is not actually gold!

My ten-day visit turns into three months, then a lifetime.

My first day in town, Lynn takes us walking across the Bridge. Then to Fisherman's Wharf, the tourist area. A sidewalk performer in face paint rides a unicycle, juggles, sings songs, and shouts jokes. Smiling tourists, crowds gathered from all corners of the world, fill his hat with money when he passes it around.

I've wandered away from Lynn; too many tourists between us. She catches my eye, smiles, points at the ice cream stand. As I wind my way through the throng to meet her, there's the performer. Sitting alone on the steps below his stage; resting before the next show. His unicycle lies on its side, wheel spinning above the earth. Up close he looks different…smoking a cigarette, unsmiling. Beneath his face paint, stubble pokes through. It's a disturbing sight…yet somehow thrilling, too.

Later, back at Uncle Jupiter's house, Lynn and I drink ginger ale in the kitchen. The side door opens. Victor makes his entrance.

He's my age and strong, a weightlifter and runner. Adidas tank top, chiseled arms. Victor's a drinker and smoker too; that odd combination of athleticism and poison-taking the young can pull off.

He carries music paper with him everywhere; he's composing a symphony.

I've read books, but Victor has read more.

"This is my cousin," Lynn says, introducing me. "From Massachusetts."

"Hi, Lynn's cousin." Victor smiles as he slips off his running shoes. "How long are you here for?"

"Ten days. If I survive. The last time I saw Lynn, I almost got alcohol poisoning." If I'd said it in the Oakmont hallways, the kids would've laughed *at* me. But Victor laughs *with* me, when I get to the part about the rabbits.

"What are you doing tonight?" He claps me on the shoulder.

I set down my ginger ale and look at Lynn.

"You two go ahead." She pulls her hair into a ponytail. "Just take care of him?"

"When's your curfew?" Victor asks.

I shrug.

"Dad wants everyone home by midnight," Lynn says. Victor's brow furrows. "Well," he breaks into a grin, turns to me, "make sure you leave the side door unlocked. You might be pretty tossed when you get home."

It's the *way he says it*. The casual implication of camaraderie and friendship. For me not to go drinking that night would have been like the ocean refusing to yield to the moon's gravitational pull. Would Victor have been my best friend that summer, even had I not learned to drink like him? Finding out was not a chance I was prepared to take.

That night we meet some others drinking on the roof of the Palace of Fine Arts. A monument modeled after Greek and Roman architecture, a popular local spot for weddings. A girl takes me off to the side. I find the courage to wrap my arms around her, hold her in an embrace. Me, the kid who couldn't find two words to say to Natalie LaFontane, holding a girl in his arms! There's tenderness between us as the San Francisco summer air chills the night.

The closeness to another human being is intoxicating.

Of course, so is the Royal Gate vodka I swill from a plastic jug.

Many years later, it's remarkable to learn how many of us in AA got started with a fine product from our friends at Royal Gate. The gate through which we stumbled into alcoholism.

On the roof of the Palace of Fine Arts, part of me arrives at a conclusion: Before a woman might allow me the warmth of her closeness, first must come warmth from a bottle. In those first few days and nights in San Francisco, I know I'm home; I know I'm never going home.

Top Gun is released that summer. Victor dreams of becoming a fighter pilot. I get caught up in his enthusiasm and decide my *goal* is to fly planes, too. After all, Victor has *confidence*. He knows a path to achieving a dream. Of course, if I'd found a friend like Victor who dreamed of becoming e a furniture-carver, an astronomer, or a bank robber? I would've traded my writer dream for the goal of fashioning a chair, peering at distant stars, pulling a John Dillinger.

You have to be in shape to be a fighter pilot. Victor teaches me to lift weights in the Presidio gym, sneaking me past the Army guard in fatigues at the front desk. Victor instructs me how to work opposing muscle groups, do push-pull routines. My muscles grow. So does my confidence. Later in life, other weight rooms become types of Cellar Holes. The gyms are places I know well enough to leap from stone to stone. There may be other humans around, but that's okay. I can tune them out enough to let my thoughts be my workout partners.

At night—nearly every night—Victor and I drink and smoke cigarettes in the parks and playgrounds. Victor works at a six-pack. I can't stomach beer; bad memories from the German festival. Instead I slug from my bottle of Royal Gate. Most nights I throw up, black out, or both.

Nothing could be more thrilling.

The kid who couldn't navigate forty feet of Oakmont hallways roaming the streets of San Francisco with a bottle of Royal Gate in one pocket of his jean jacket, a pack of Camels in the other. Towards the end of the summer, Victor quits drinking and moves to San Diego to be closer to the Miramar military flight school. He realizes alcohol stands between him and his dreams.

Me, I've put my dream off to the side. *Drinking makes me feel normal.* It's a good enough substitute for becoming a writer. In San Francisco, I've had my first kiss, my first experience of what felt like true freedom. Booze has been there all the while.

Flying a plane? An adopted goal. If it gets in the way of drinking, it's easy to let slip away.

The summer ends. I drag myself back to Ashburnham. In Oakmont, I'm on a path to acceptance: Through drinking. And, thanks to the weightlifting, I'm a prospect for the football team (at Oakmont, being on the football team is like serving on the elite Praetorian Guard in the days of Caesar).

But having had a taste of freedom, I can't accept a small town's confinement. At home I throw tantrums, scream at my dad, break dishes at the round wooden dining table. No roaming San Francisco to burn off negative energy. I'm a hulking, sullen presence around the house. Rage and bitterness from the Oakmont bullying wells up. I direct it at the most available targets: my parents. I'd been too much like my parents to fit in at Oakmont. Now I'm too much like the kids at school to fit in with my parents. I barely speak to Blossom. At night I shut myself away in my bedroom. My mind is on the roof of the Palace of Fine Arts. I make no effort to hide my new cigarette habit, ducking out behind the barn after dinner to suck down Camels. My mom got into an anti-smoking campaign when I was a kid. She carried a handbag with a slogan: "Smoking Stinks."

Before I'd left for my summer in San Francisco, I'd done well on the standardized academic tests. My high school grades haven't yet begun to slide. When I apply for early acceptance to the University of San Francisco, my application is approved.

Salvation, or so it seems. I'll be leaving high school after my junior year.

A few years back, Mark Burnsen moved to Ashburnham. Being the new kid and not knowing any better than to hang out with the loser, he hangs out with me. Mark's not the kind who cares much about popularity anyway. We organize pickup football games. I'm in a three-point stance and look up to see Mark about to run out for a pass with a lit cigarette dangling from his lips.

He'll catch the pass, too. Probably score a touchdown.

Mark's wiry and strong, big biceps hoist his BMX bike into a wheelie, and he rides it out as long as he wants. The girls like him, yet he seems not to notice (that's probably why they like him). He plays drums like Neil Peart (Rush is one of the few bands you can listen to at Oakmont if you don't want to be scoffed at—along with Ozzy, Van Halen, Led Zeppelin, a few others). Mark doesn't care; his favorite band is the Cars. He could make any sports team, but he doesn't try out for any. He's smart, too. In the upper-level classes; sits near me in Latin and algebra.

I spend my last summer in Ashburnham with Mark and his friends. Hanging out around the lake near his house. Waterskiing, swimming, playing volleyball. At night we drink at a home where the parents are away.

Mark dates Tess. One night she brings her friend Frankie to a party. Frankie is a local girl, innocent and smart. She and I ride in my red Ford pickup to a place atop the hill on the town line. There's a four-story water tower, with "Welcome to Ashburnham, Mass" painted in giant letters on the side. We park in the woods. Frankie tells me what she wants from me, before she'll give me what I want from her.

"What should I do?" I ask Mark the next day. We're smoking cigarettes, wearing shorts and t-shirts in the Massachusetts humidity, walking along the dirt road that winds along the lake.

"What do you want to do?"

"I want to have sex," I say, thinking it's true. "But she says I have to tell her I love her."

A motorboat cruise the lake, towing a waterskier. The skier slashes across the wake and takes to the air.

"Don't tell her you love her if you don't."

"How else will I have sex with her?" I kick a rock, sending

Three: Weddings

it off into a patch of ferns.

"You probably won't." Mark grins, flicks his cigarette ash. "There'll be other opportunities, dude."

The motorboat makes a sweeping turn. The skier tries another jump. But his angle is wrong, or there's too much slack in the towline. He crashes under the surface.

Having sex with Frankie is a goal. Like piloting a fighter plane. I may not be drunk when Frankie and I sleep together in her parents' empty house, but I've lied to her. Told her I loved her. For me, the truth extends to the point of satisfying short-term base desires. Not much further.

A few nights later, I drive my pickup truck through downtown Ashburnham, stopping in the dead quiet of the parking lot near the town hall. The stone steps of the public library off to my left. I can't remember the last time I climbed those steps. My friends sleep inside. Characters from Blume, Tolkien, Hinton. I am a character, woven from lies, fantasies, adopting others' goals as my own.

I punch the truck in gear, peel out of the parking lot. Driving to escape Ashburnham…it seems like the best thing I can do, given where my choices are leading me. The next day, my plane takes off for San Francisco.

Four:

Lies

...the best things we do so often carry seeds of one's own destruction.

—Toni Morrison

I turn the key and throw open the door. Not knowing better than to knock first. Logan is alone. All I'm interrupting is his nap. I enter my dorm room at the University of San Francisco. Meet my new roommate for the first time.

"Hey, man," Logan says. Maybe I've woken him from a dream. "What's going on?"

"I guess this is my room." I drop my suitcase, the clothes and few books it contains.

"It's our room, buddy." He grins and sits up. "I tried to call you over the summer. The school wouldn't give me your phone number. Wouldn't even tell me your name. How are you supposed to find out who your roommate is?"

"You got me." I look around. The room may be small, but it's freedom. A window takes up the length of the longest wall. The view of the San Francisco skyline you'd pay to have on a postcard. The Transamerica Pyramid, the triangular skyscraper, like a ladder connecting Earth to Heaven.

Four: Lies

College dorm room...you can move across a continent, but where you moved from may follow you

"I wanted to ask you what you were bringing." Logan swings his legs over the bed, stands at his six-foot-four height. "My mom made sure we're okay. I got us a stereo. A mini fridge. A television." He points. A stereo on a shelf is piled with cassette tapes, mostly eighties metal. "I got everything we need." There's a box of Hostess donuts next to a TV with its antenna pointed towards outer space.

"All I brought are books," I say. "And a couple of pennants." The pennants have logos of the New England teams: Celtics, Patriots, Red Sox.

"That's cool," he says, smiling. "I have everything we need."

I take out a cigarette. "Mind if I smoke?" I search my pockets for matches, can't find any.

"Go ahead," he says. "It's our room."

I open the window. San Francisco downtown has a whiteish look. The Transamerica Pyramid stabs at the sky like an ivory dagger. You get closer, and the colors change. Like the street performer on Fisherman's Wharf, stubble under his makeup.

"Want a beer?" Logan pops open the mini fridge. There's a double row of bottles of Miller Genuine Draft. He hauls out two.

"Did your mom buy you those?"

He laughs. "My mom is chill. Not that chill."

As the Pyramid office lights glitter against darkening skies, Logan and I drink. We compare backgrounds. He went to high school in Holland—his father is an international businessman. He starred on his basketball team, if not in his academic pursuits. His dad got transferred; Logan spent his senior year in New Jersey. He starred on the basketball team there. He dated a cheerleader. To say Logan is worldly and mature in comparison to me is like describing the Guggenheim as having slightly superior architecture to the cement curb onto which one steps in order to reach the entrance.

"So," he says, "what's your story?"

My story?

I want Logan to like me. If Frankie had sex with me because I lied to her, it stands to reason Logan will be my friend if I lie to him.

"I played football in high school," I lie.

"Really?" He swigs his beer-dregs. I follow suit, scowling at the bitter warmth.

"Yeah, my senior year was the best. I had a girlfriend...she wasn't a cheerleader, but, you know, she said she loved me."

Logan goes for the fridge. Hands me a bottle, takes one for himself.

"Oh, yeah...and I'm a writer." I pop the top of my Miller.

Four: Lies

"A writer?" Logan looks impressed. "That's cool. Maybe you can help me write my papers."

We host parties in our room every Thursday night. Logan blasts the stereo: Ratt, Whitesnake, Def Leppard. Eighties heavy metal screams through Phelan Residence Hall, while off in the distance the Transamerica Pyramid stands like a chess rook watching over his queen. Logan and I get a bright idea: His mom bought him desk supplies, including a stapler. We staple empty Miller Genuine Draft cardboard six-pack holders to the dorm room ceiling. The cardboard is black, so the ceiling looks like it's five feet above the floor.

Students from the Culinary Academy live in dorm rooms down the hall. They bring bags of weed to our parties. Someone teaches me how to wedge a bottle cap between my index finger and thumb, point my elbow, and snap my fingers, launching the bottle cap like a missile. Like the boomerang-knife wielded by the kid in *The Road Warrior*. Any bottlecap-rocket is bound to hit someone. Our room is jam-packed with partygoers…

Many of them female.

In those less enlightened times? A college freshman's overt purpose of drunken sexual encounters, categorized the freshman differently than it does today (at least, let's hope things are different today). There are meaningless physical encounters with women. Surrounded by empty six-pack holders and moldy pizza boxes, a dart board for drinking games hung on the door, young women and I mash our lips and bodies together. Rarely do we have sex. Instead, there's groping, longing, curiosity satisfied to a surface-level point, stopping well short of commitment.

There's one semi-relationship. Phyllis is a couple years older, an art student and long-distance runner. There's a strange time when she tells me she's pregnant after we had unprotected sex in her parents' hot tub. She decided on an abortion, without telling me. Then confesses she lied about the whole story. I don't much question her actions. *This is how life goes.* The kind of rock-solid self-respect platform the problem drinker builds under his or her life.

One afternoon Phyllis finds me on the quad. She hands me a note. "Don't read it now," she says. "Save it."

Later, in class, as the professor recounts a Revolutionary War battle, I unfold the note. *This is gonna be about how much she loves me.* Surprise! She's breaking up with me. I race to her apartment to try and change her mind. The best I can get is a drive in her Oldsmobile. We park on the Presidio, overlooking the Golden Gate Bridge. I'm sobbing, my head in her lap, begging her to take me back. But it's no use.

I sink into a months-long depression. I've lost the one love of my life. Nothing can ever be right again. I drive Logan crazy the rest of the semester, moping around.

In 1982, USF student and basketball star Quintin Dailey, who went on to play for the Chicago Bulls, was arrested for sexual assault. The school shut down the men's basketball program. To maintain the NCAA divisional status (they needed to have a certain number of men's teams), they added crew.

Logan goes out for the team. With his height and athleticism, he's a natural rower.

Me? Different story.

Four: Lies

Yet I adopt Logan's goal and go out for crew team too. It's sheer madness, really. Practices are Saturday and Sunday at seven in the morning. I could be in the library, pursuing a degree in English or creative writing. Instead I'm hung over, dragging myself across the water in a crew shell behind Logan.

Logan has a dream: to become a mature adult, having learned from and enjoyed his college experience. His dream shapes his goals: Make the crew team, pass his classes, socialize.

I write a story or two. Professors compliment my essays and papers. I tell myself, *They're just being nice.* Somehow I've convinced myself to take up writing and not be considered the greatest living writer is a waste of time. It's not enough to write a journal or a letter to the editor of the USF newspaper; I must compose a screenplay that wins an Oscar, a novel that outsells Bret Easton Ellis.

I tell myself the reason not to pursue an English degree is that writing shouldn't be a job. I want it to be my hobby, not something I'm forced to do. But it doesn't become my hobby, either.

The truth behind why I don't pursue my dream?

The writer I wish to become, is not *me as a writer.*

I long to become a *completely different person.*

To transform into a character from the Cellar Hole, or from my lies.

This is why I get intoxicated. Not to be a drunk/high version of myself. I want to turn myself into someone *completely different.* There aren't enough drinks or drugs in the world to do that.

When I'm not drinking, I drift deeper into fantasy. No longer am I—in my fantasies—the kid who has something to say to Natalie LaFontane at the locker next to mine. I've become (in my mind) a martial arts expert. Unafraid to stand up to bullies, able to defeat the staunchest opponent with a *knife-hand death throw*, my signature blow (I don't actually kill anyone, even in my imagination). I dream myself into a sensational tailback on the USF football team. In reality, USF doesn't even have a football team. I imagine myself a virtuoso rock guitarist, on stage with Eddie Van Halen, admired by women and envied by men. Leading drunken masses in revelry from the stage of the Fog n' Grog, the campus watering hole.

No matter where I go or what I'm doing, in my mind I'm somewhere else.

Someone else.

One Thursday night, Logan and I roam the Phelan hallways. Wearing sunglasses, for some reason. Logan is on crutches—he went in for a tackle in a pickup football game on the campus quad and slid into a post, breaking his leg (USF expelled the post). We wander into a room. Culinary Academy guys sit around a mini stack of milk crates that serves as a table. A future chef whips up a different kind of recipe: He pours white powder onto a mirror and offers me a rolled-up bill.

Once, in the Oakmont High School cafeteria, I overheard Corey Hillman talking about cocaine. Even in sixth grade, Corey wore shirts open to the waist and had perfect hair. He liked you to know his status as a swinging ladies' man. Always describing these sexual encounters he had, of remarkable variety and frequency. His mom sent him to the supermarket for a gallon of milk—a shelf-stocker lured him into the storeroom and shed her blouse. Corey *projected confidence.* Kids crowded around to hear him talk, like we inmates crowded around Deputy Horne's baseball card.

Until the night when Logan and I, wearing sunglasses, wandered into the room where Culinary Academy guys snorted lines? I'd only lied about having done coke. Thinking it would make a part of a special club. It will end up doing that, all right.

"What's it like?" Logan asks me. His sunglasses are perched on his head as he crutches alongside me along the Phelan hallway.

"It's different than the other stuff I've done." In truth, the coke makes my mind feel like a chainsaw after someone ripped the starter cord. I am *alive,* like the top of the Transamerica pyramid is *below me.* Like my mind is a battleship radar screen, able to detect what before was invisible.

Soon enough, the *cocaine high*—as you'll see—becomes too much. But the *cocaine lifestyle*...it's almost like my fantasy version of myself becomes real. While I never let loose with a knife-hand death throw, the cokehead lifestyle lets me feel like *I am somebody.*

At a party, taking someone aside and saying, "Wanna do a line?" It's back to being that kid on the roof of the Palace of Fine Arts, or at the German beer festival. *I'm the person who knows how to get high.* I imagine it's the feeling of saying, "I'm a writer," and having it be the truth.

Cocaine has side effects. One night I'm holed up in my dorm room, afraid to go to the common bathroom. Ashamed my fellow students will see how high I am. I pee in a beer can and drop it out the fourth-floor window. These types of things become as routine as the reading assignments I don't do.

One night, after too many lines, drinks, and bong hits, my heart begins beating wildly, out of control. Panic sets in as the various poisons bubble through my system. Logan sits by the side of my bed, watching over me. No ambulances are called, no emergency room visited. But from that night forward, coke binges start surrounded by friends. With big plans for the best of times. Those binges end with me in bed, trying to stave off what I'm sure is a heart attack. No stopping my heart from stopping, seconds from cardiac arrest…lying on my left side, like I read somewhere is the recovery position from heart attack…more blood to the pump, better chance of survival. Cardiac rhythm racing, aortic explosion imminent, desperate to delay the dying and chunks of my heart rotting. Fighting to hold my breathing steady, keep my heart beating a few more minutes.

Then there's the matter of police paranoia. With the cocaine blitz comes teams of officers assembled outside the front door. Helicopters, SWAT teams readying to rappel through the windows. White vans cruise the streets, preparing to unload a phalanx of cops to smash into my bedroom and drag me away. Rising from bed to peep through the keyhole and jump at shadows. Hearing what I'm sure are the neighbors' voices talking about me. Never able to understand what they say.

There's too the matter your serious coke binger knows and comprehends…the soul-crushing self-hatred, when dawn creeps silently through the bedroom Venetian blinds and the previous night's friends and revelry—so important just hours before—are nothing more than a jumble of hazy memories, less real than a dream. The bulk of yet another week's paycheck is spent on a small fold of magazine paper, the white powder it once contained, gone, the paper licked clean as a cat's paw, despite the previous night's certainty *it's not gonna happen again, not this time.* Yet it happened! Again. And now I lie sleepless, any thoughts of my worth as a human scrubbed from my mind. Clinging desperately to the flimsy reed of an idea that *as of now, I'm quit for good*…laughable, were it not for the planet-like weight of the cocaine misery.

Before every binge I swear: *Tonight, it will be different.* There will be no succumbing to the paranoia of heart attacks and police. Instead, a couple of lines, a few drinks, asleep by 2:00 a.m. Yet dawn finds me back in the same headspace, wondering, *What happened?* I always believe the drugs can be kept under control…more willpower, all that's needed. *It should be easy!* Yet when it comes to cocaine, the subconscious works against forms of reasoning. Sure, before I snort that first line, there's the subconscious certainty I'll wind up in the recovery position waiting for SWAT team helicopters to land on the roof. But there's another subconscious certainty: *I can survive.* I can make it to the other side. I've done it before, many times.

Pursuit of my dream of being a writer? Huh. No telling where that may end up….

It's a crisp sunny day when Chester drops by our dorm room. Chester is an esoteric type of associate, the kind we in the drug world tend to discover. He deals coke, rides a superbike, likes to drop acid and go lift weights at the USF gym. He's buffed out, chiseled, strong legs and arms. You'd see him in the weight room with hundreds of pounds over his head and who knows what inside his mind.

Chester produces a baggie from inside his motorcycle jacket. "It's called glass," he says, holding it up to the sunlight.

"What, like speed?"

He shrugs. "You don't have to do much. A little is all you need."

Chester grins and removes the *Batman* soundtrack CD case from the stereo rack. "I think CDs were invented to do drugs on the cases." He crushes the glass with a credit card and hands it to me.

There's no question I'll do it. An acid-dropping coke dealer pulls up on his Kawasaki Ninja at ten o'clock on a Saturday morning? For me not to partake in whatever happens next would be like going back to being the high-school loser haunting the Oakmont hallways. Drugs make me part of a special club. This morning is no exception.

The first line feels like sticking a flare gun in my nostril and pulling the trigger. When the pain subsides, I feel like a superman, a hero. Like I've become the person I tell everyone I am. The football player, the guitarist, the martial arts expert… yes, even the writer. All I have to do now, is write.

But first, maybe another line…

Five:

Poem

The wise do not need counsel, and fools will not take it.

—Seneca

As a maturing member of the USF drinking crowd, I begin drinking at Pat O'Shea's on Thursday nights. The bartenders draw draught pints as local sports legends gaze towards bleachers in autographed black-and-whites hanging from the walls. I'm wearing a Ralph Lauren shirt, khakis, and Nikes, and my hair is short. On my wrist, my father's Rolex. A beautiful silver-and-stainless-steel Oyster. I swear I'll wear it forever. I drain my greyhound—vodka and grapefruit juice—and look for a waitress to bring another.

Instead, there's Poem.

"Hey! Aren't you the guy with the motorcycle?" Poem wears a flower-print jacket, and her hair is dark brown with streaks of blonde. "I saw you riding up to Lone Mountain campus. How come you didn't give me a ride?"

"Um…I thought you wanted to climb all those steps to have a thirst to quench." I nod at the pint of beer she holds.

"I only drink on days ending in Y!"

Similar erudite banter ensues. Real college talk, the stuff of debate teams. Made bold by the greyhounds, I ask Poem if she wants that motorcycle ride. "I know a place with a great view of the church," I tell her.

That place is my bedroom. You can see the floodlit USF church at the top of its hill. Poem and I kneel on my mattress on the floor, gazing out the window. We make out. She falls asleep, and I creep into the living room to snort coke by myself. The cycle, with slight variations, repeats itself for the next four years.

One day Poem calls me. "You *have to* come over." She gets this dead serious, matter-of-fact way of talking. "You *won't believe* what I've found." She waits outside her apartment as I pull up on my motorcycle. Next to her, there's this couch—used, not unsalvageable. The first thing you notice is how long it is. Like someone took two couches, tore an armrest off each, and stuck them together.

"Look!" She throws her arms around me and plants a kiss. "Someone was just giving it away!"

"Poem…this thing is as long as an Apollo rocket."

"I know! Isn't it great?"

"How are you going to get it upstairs?"

Her eyes narrow. "You mean, how are *we* going to get it upstairs." She leaps onto the cushions. "It's so comfortable! C'mon, try it."

I sit down. "Sure." I look up at her apartment. "But how…"

"We'll figure it out," she says, kissing me again. "Just you watch."

An hour later, she's called over two friends. We're wrestling the couch up the stairs.

"Are you sure it won't work?" Poem looks over the

bannister at me.

"It won't go any further! The corner, it won't turn."

"It's okay! I have some rope."

"Rope?"

"We'll get it in through the window."

"But…the only window big enough is in the back of the building."

If you happened to be driving down Stanyan Street in San Francisco sometime in 1990 and saw what looked like a church pew with armrests dangling against the side of a building, this is why. Now you know. We hoist the couch up one side of the building, not coming too close to dropping it on some unsuspecting tourists on their way to Golden Gate Park. We carry it across the roof, lower it down the other side. Poem uses a claw hammer to tear away the window frame from the inside.

"I think it's gonna work out!" she shouts. "I really do!"

We'll spend a lot of nights on that couch. Up past dawn, following nights in the bars surrounded by smiling friends and handsome, well-dressed strangers. Bartenders quick with jokes and cocktail glasses like the sun's rays glinting off the ocean. We hold each other on that couch, whispering, "I love you." For many years it's the furthest I'll get from those words being a lie.

Poem sits behind the wheel of my silver Toyota Corolla. The car was a college graduation present from my parents. Uncle Jupiter sold it to them (at full Blue Book value). I'm wearing work clothes: a Ralph Lauren shirt, tie, khakis. My father's Rolex. Poem leaves me on the corner of 7th and Townsend Street. It's eight in the morning.

"Have a good first day at work!" she sings. "I'll be back at five. Don't worry if you get held up. I can find a way to occupy myself." I cross the train tracks, watching her drive away. Above me, the five-story brick structure where the temp agency told me to find the offices of Interaction Associates. The morning sky is cloudy.

It's January 1992. The previous May, by some miracle, USF awarded me a diploma. My parents visited me for the first time. I showed them around, playing the big shot in my new hometown, even though I'd lived in San Francisco over four years. What college kids do when the parents visit. The child now become the adult (the parents still pick up the tab, of course).

I spun like a sun; my family members were orbiting planets. The unfathomable distance between us filled with the dark matter of my cocaine addiction. When we spin close to each other's orbits, I have my protective fields of moons and meteor belts: lies, crutches, appearances. Ralph Lauren clothes and short hair. Part-time jobs and afternoons in the gym. All of it designed to construct a facade. *Look, family, here's your kid who doesn't have a drug problem.* And the people…Logan, Poem… in front of my family, they make me not guilty by association.

A month or so after graduation, I moved to Albuquerque.

Victor lived there. I planned to become a writer.

I packed all my things into the silver Toyota. Including my paperback book collection. The weight must've been a nightmare on fuel consumption, but I didn't know any better. I piloted across the desert. You hear of addicts pulling a "geographic." Taking our physical bodies somewhere, hoping our mental states will remain behind. In Albuquerque, I got

Five: Poem

a job driving a truck for a lumber company. Payday every Friday. A bank across the street from the lumberyard cashed my check. I headed for the bar across the street from the bank. By midnight, most of my earnings were gone to Wild Turkey.

Poem and I talked on the phone, wrote letters. I tried to enchant her, a thousand miles away, with outlines of the novel I'd drafted in my mind. I missed her when she was away. I'd taken her for granted when we were close.

I'd run from cocaine; Wild Turkey and weed took its place. My problems followed across the desert...*I was still me.* I couldn't even think of myself as a *failed* writer. I'd never even *tried* to write. Not in any meaningful way. At one point, I'd called my father. A week or so after I'd told my landlord my father was dead, as an excuse for breaking the lease early.

"Dad, I'm heading back to San Francisco. I want to write."

"Well," he said, "there's something to be said for just holing up and writing."

All I needed to hear! I hadn't become a writer—it must be *Albuquerque's fault.* But back in San Francisco, Logan worked a professional job. It seemed like what I should do, too. Never mind my dad's advice. The goal of a landing a professional job was easier than the pursuit of my dream.

I threw together a resume, called a temporary staffing agency. That's how I arrive at Interaction Associates. IA is a management consulting company. They help clients foster collaborative, mutually respectful environments in meetings and on teams. In my khakis and tie, I don't exactly fit in with IA's culture. My soon-to-be colleagues are writers, musicians, artists, gay men. Despite having lived in San Francisco four years, I have no gay friends. IA changes that.

Rockman and I smoke weed on the IA fire escapes. We're joined by Henry, a speed-metal drummer who administers the computer systems. We have old Macs with integrated monitor and hard drive, Netscape email with no spell check.

Rockman lives in a cottage in the Castro and brings me to the gay bars. I don't feel uncomfortable, and hopefully my presence as a straight guy doesn't make anyone else uncomfortable (of course, that only occurs to me years later—never at the time). As bass music pounds and Rockman orders us beers, I think about how the men surrounding me could physically overpower me if they wanted to. Is this part of what it feels like to be a woman? Forced to live with the constant potential of physical threat? Sometimes I think, *I'd be gay, if I could.* If I could somehow make it so I find men as physically attractive as women. I've never had a homosexual experience, never been curious to. Never felt the need to condemn anyone for being gay. I think about the stigma homosexuals are forced to endure. I know about a kind of stigma. Plenty of people would condemn me for the drugs I do. Yet doing drugs is a choice, right?

During the week, I exercise and work. Long bicycle rides across the Golden Gate Bridge. Hours spent weightlifting. Home, and straight to the marijuana bong and pizza delivery. Long hours at the office. Time spent with supervisors, mentors, colleagues. Then snorting coke all night on a Tuesday, calling in sick on Wednesday.

The morning after a coke binge…alone, afraid to go outside, too ashamed of how high I let myself get, the depths to which

Five: Poem

I let myself sink. Another hundred dollars spent. Another night of marathon masturbation in my room. Almost as many mornings as I've faced in this condition have there been that many times I swore never again to snort coke. Every following weekend, the cycle repeats.

Drug addiction is a condition of comfort.
As an addict, I'm comfortable in the throes of a binge.
I know this place. It is familiar.
Lying in the recovery position, paranoid, waiting for the SWAT team to kick down my door? I'm not happy, but *comfort does not equal happiness.* In prehistoric times, our ancestors who found comfort in the cave's darkness—afraid to leave at night, instead groping for companions sharing animal-skin blankets as the cooking fire crackled and sparked its final life—were the ones to survive. To pass along genes. Those who explored the forests by moonlight? Eaten by tigers, plunged from cliffs.

In modern times we lie awake. Watchful as our surviving ancestors. Yet with our physical existence no longer in question, we find ourselves gripped by different kinds of fears. Our survival minds, evolved through millennia to solve solid problems such as how to eat, how not to be eaten? Instead churn out answers to dilemmas that can't be solved.

In 1996, there's a rave scene in San Francisco. Underground dance parties with names like Five-Foot Tongue, Glass House, and ToonTown. Held in different locations from weekend to weekend. To find one you have to be in the know.

I'm not in the know.
I don't dance much, or well.

But I do start using meth. Regular-like.

Cocaine—the heart attacks and paranoia—has become too hard on me.

I score meth (we're still calling it speed back then) from a couple of club-goers. Soon I've quit my job, figuring I'll be quitting my problems, too. On my last day of work, my uniform is jeans, motorcycle boots, and a black hooded sweatshirt. I've dyed my hair bright blonde and grown a ponytail. I have my first visible tattoo: The cover art from *Fear & Loathing in Las Vegas*, my favorite book. Hunter S. Thompson, the author, desperate to avoid his pursuers, sneaking away after running up a fantastic hotel bill he can't possibly pay. For years, the caricature of Thompson is all I ever wanted to be: an author with access to all the drugs he couldn't handle.

During my time at IA, the first thirty pages of a novel I compose are little more than a ripoff of *Fear & Loathing*. It's all the writing I'd done in five years. When you average it out? About half a page a month. A sentence a day. How long does it take to write a sentence? I wrote that last one in fifteen seconds. Less time than it takes to fill a pot pipe or chop a line of speed.

Poem? Gone from my life. She was good to me…like everyone in my life who treats me well, I resent her for it. *I know the real me.* And deep inside, I assume everyone else does, too. If you're good to me, you must either be stupid or be out to get me. *There cannot be any other reasons.*

Poem finds another boyfriend. Of course, I start wanting her back. Depression sets in, same as it did with Phyllis, the USF art student. I make myself miserable, wanting who I can't have. I'm comfortable being miserable…unhappiness is my default state. Loneliness is the best-known feeling, if not the best liked.

Comfort does not equal happiness.

Poem goes on to a nice life, getting married and raising kids, becoming a successful corporate executive. I'll choose another marriage. It's 1996, and I've become a methamphetamine addict.

Six:
Bangkok

All us boxing people realize evening is here and night will soon befall us.

—Muhammad Ali

The summit of Mount Fuji appears below me. Like the top of the Transamerica Pyramid. I've slept off a speed binge, slid the screen from the fuselage window.

You could balance a plank on the tip of Mount Fuji. Make a seesaw.

A seesaw. What my life is like in November 2000.

On one side: The Biotech Giant, kickboxing, the rest of it.

On the other side: Drugs.

After Interaction Associates, I spent a couple months as a bike messenger. It didn't interfere with getting high. The messengers congregated at the Wall, a stone structure at Sansome and Sutter Streets. Smoking grass in the sunshine of the Financial District's beating heart. Made me feel like one of the popular kids at Oakmont. It's an experience one might write a book about. I daydreamed about doing just that, cradling my wooden pot pipe. But my bike—a critical component of bike messengering—got stolen. And I couldn't pay the rent

Six: Bangkok

on a messenger's salary.

A friend landed me a temp job with the Biotech Giant. First Monday, no sleep the night before. Still jacked from partying on speed all weekend. Riding BART, jittery, anxious. Feeling other riders staring at me all the way to Glen Park Station.

And then, gliding up curbside, near the grassy valley where goats roam wild, a shuttle bus. Spotless, plush seats, plenty of legroom. The bus is a free amenity, to ferry workers to the Giant. A quiet ride and almost-nap later, I'm in the offices, which will be home for the next five years.

"Want an espresso?" my supervisor asks me before assigning me any work. "They're free! There's a machine in the breakroom."

At first, I work on a project meant to end cystic fibrosis. CF steals children's lives, robs them of their youth. They can't run and play, with the breathing difficulties, lung infections, coughing. My writing ability impresses my managers. Assignments follow: create a newsletter for doctors and nursing professionals; construct PowerPoint presentations (not the kind on jailhouse notebook paper, either) and manuscripts for medical journals. Basic stuff, editing and copywriting. It made me happy to help kids with CF and their parents.

Not only is the espresso free, the Giant has onsite catering for noon meetings. Always leftovers, if you don't mind waiting. I don't mind. They have these brownies, like sticks of butter with chocolate flavoring.

Working for the Biotech Giant makes my soul and stomach happy. It makes Uncle Jupiter happy. He can't be expected to believe what he thinks is good for me might not be good for me. Sunday dinners and Passover Seders at Jupiter's, I tell the odd joke. Slip in a remark or two about getting a bonus check, a pay raise. Mention hitting the gym four out of five days this week. Put up a good front for the drugs to lurk behind.

My mom mails clippings from the *New York Times* about the Giant's accomplishments. I never read them. My interest is helping kids with CF. If a short story or a book I'd written got mentioned in the *Times*? I'd have wallpapered my home with clippings. Like those black cardboard six-pack holders Logan and I stapled to our dorm room ceiling.

A friend introduces me to the Fairtex school of Muay Thai (kickboxing). A gym like you find in the fighting world; you train there for the community as much as to learn kicks and strikes. Maybe more so. Fairtex instructors are mostly Thai, moved here from Southeast Asia. They live in an apartment upstairs from the training floor. Old-school style.

A certain instructor drifts in to Fairtex every so often. Cheetah was a Muay Thai champion in his native Thailand. He has a powerful body and a handsome, chiseled face. As you might guess, he didn't get his nickname by fighting at a snail's pace.

"You have some skills." Cheetah takes me aside one night after sparring class. His speech is soft, gentle, not in keeping with a guy who could knock you into next week anytime he halfway feels like it. "You should take private lessons. Push yourself to the next level."

On Saturday mornings in 2000, my routine is to ride my BMW motorcycle (the bike was my father's; he had it shipped cross-country to me) across the Bay Bridge for private lessons with Cheetah. Training is a bare-bones, spartan affair.

Six: Bangkok

Jump-roping barefoot on the cement floors. No hot water in the shower. A pro fighter once told me Muay Thai started as a way to figure out: *Who's the toughest guy?* Whether old-time fighters coated their knuckles in broken glass, as the stories go, is a matter of debate. But you can watch Muay Thai fights on YouTube and see for yourself; Bangkok pros don't mind trading a few kicks and punches.

As an addict, I train with Cheetah because it isn't enough to kickbox for the sake of enjoyment, or for keeping in shape. I am driven to devote untold hours, strive to become an amateur fighter. Sure, part of me wants to evolve into the martial arts phenomenon from my college fantasies with the knife-hand death throw. Yet the other facet to Muay Thai obsession is the same story you find with a lot of addicts.

Training fifteen hours a week at Muay Thai? Not something a drug addict would do. *Right?* Therefore, if I train that much, I must not be a drug addict.

Or so I convince myself.

Never mind every Saturday I go straight from the cold shower to the speed.

A meth connect lives in a house near a hilltop. We lose entire weekends in his living room, snorting lines, smoking grass and cigarettes, drinking beer. Watching pornos. I go home to masturbate and smoke bong hits in my room all Sunday. Monday mornings find me in my cubicle at the Biotech Giant. Taking the lead on projects, doing extra work, setting myself apart. Again, not the things a drug addict does, right?

A seesaw. What my life is like in November 2000.

One Saturday morning, post-workout and cold shower, I'm

ready to hop on my BMW and two-wheel it across the bridge for another binge weekend. Cheetah stops me. "Hey, Champ," his soft voice says. *Champ* is his nickname for me. Probably meant in jest (I'm so good at kickboxing that I can, at will, hit my opponent's fist with any part of my face). "I'm organizing another trip to Thailand." Thailand tours are Cheetah's side endeavor. He wants me along on the next one.

That's how I wake from sleeping off another speed binge...

The summit of Mount Fuji appears below me. Like the top of the Transamerica Pyramid.

A couple days later, it's Thanksgiving. Cheetah occupies the head of our table in the Karnmanee Palace Hotel in Bangkok (today their website advertises "Free bike for rent"). We wolf down Thanksgiving dinners of sticky rice and *Pad Thai*. Home in the States, George Bush and Al Gore battle to see who will be president. We seven Californians have spent the past couple day touring the temples; are now making plans for the next leg.

"So," Cheetah's gentle voice says, "everybody ready to go to Chiang Mai?"

"Where is Chiang Mai?" I ask.

"It's in the north."

"I'm not going," Caesar declares flatly. Caesar is a Muay Thai trainer himself, one of Cheetah's disciples. A family man with a direct manner and focused determination. "I want to train in the camp," he says.

"The camp?" Christoph asks, incredulous. Christoph has a bodybuilder's physique and is quick to smile and laugh. The "camp" is where young Thai men live while they attend school

Six: Bangkok

and train to fight in the Muay Thai stadiums. Cheetah had brought us for a quick visit the day before.

Caesar drains his water glass. "You guys go on to Chiang Mai. I'm gonna go to camp. I'm here to train, to learn."

Christoph shrugs, smiles. "Sounds good to me. I'm going with you." His grin gets wider as his gaze settles on me. He claps me on the shoulder. "You're coming with us to camp, right?"

I wince, choke on my sticky rice. Feeling like the only soldier in line who doesn't take two steps backward when the drill sergeant orders a volunteer take two steps forward. Training at camp is supposed to be intense, the fighters some of the best and toughest in the world. How much sympathy would they show an overfed American like me? But something about the conviction Caesar and Christoph display strikes me. There's a sense of adventure, of challenge.

"Cheetah," I say, swallowing hard. "Is it okay if I stay behind and go to camp, too?"

Cheetah smiles. "Okay, Champ."

"Okay," Caesar says, rising from his chair. "So, it's settled. I'm gonna go upstairs and pack."

"Yeah," Christoph says. "Me, too."

"You guys go ahead," I say. "I'll join you." I sit a little longer at the table as Cheetah and the rest of the group tell stories about Chiang Mai—its beauty, the hundreds of Buddhist temples there. The way they describe it, it almost sounds like Heaven.

"I am from France," Omar says, sitting up from his afternoon nap. Caesar, Christoph, and I have barged into his room at the Muay Thai camp.

"We're from California," one of us had said, as if it explained anything.

The camp headmistress had showed us to the room the four of us will share. Until we Californians arrived, Omar had it to himself. Yet he's good-natured about it.

"I am from France." He rises from his cot, pushes a button on a boom box. Through the course of the next six days he'll play the same two hip-hop tunes over and over. Tracks off *Born to Do It,* Craig David's album. On a clothes rack Omar's hung his knockoff Ralph Lauren shirts, bought for a few *bhat* in the Bangkok markets.

He instructs us on the camp routine. "Tomorrow is Sunday," he says. "A holiday." With his French accent, it sounds like *holy day.* "Today we make the run." He reaches for his sneakers and looks at me. "You can run?"

I open my duffle bag, the one I packed high on meth back in San Francisco, and search for my own running shoes.

We make the run mornings and afternoons. The Thai fighters—young men whose physical conditioning makes Olympic athletes look like retirees snoozing poolside—leave camp first. Omar and I follow. He knows the routes through Bangkok's maze of streets. The winter heat is not as intense as other times of the year. The morning run lasts an hour. Caesar can't run due to a knee injury. Christoph gets heat stroke the first day of training; collapses on the cement training floor. The Thai fighters see this happen with foreigners. They know what to do.

"Don't worry," Omar tells me as the Thais fan the prostrate Christoph with towels and pour ice down the front of his

Six: Bangkok

shorts. "Your friend will be fine." Indeed, Christoph rises, as if from the dead, a few minutes later. He'll train hard the rest of the week but won't run with us.

Omar and I make the run alone together through the tangled Bangkok streets. Pollution hangs in the air like a glove about to be slipped over fingers formed by intersecting alleys. Despite the drugs I've been doing back in San Francisco, my conditioning is good. Yet not as good as Omar's. He runs ahead of me. Always ahead. At one point we cruise along a wide boulevard. Bustling Thais in t-shirts and flip-slops crowd the sidewalk—too many to run amongst. Omar side-steps, so he's in the roadway. I follow. Cars, trucks, and motorcycles flash past. Little but faith between us and speeding hunks of metal and churning gasoline. But I trust Omar. From time to time he looks back over his shoulder. When he sees me lagging behind, he waves for me to go faster, to keep up.

We re-enter camp, bowing to the Head Master. He's confined to wheelchair. Old fighting injuries, maybe. He makes an appearance only to sit in the doorway and see us back from making the run. The Thai fighters seem to enjoy our presence, and the training is not as brutal as we expected. It's more like what I imagine a fantasy camp to be. Thai trainers hold pads for me to throw round kicks. The fighters show me combinations against heavy bags swinging like corpses. I experience how professionals train in Bangkok, the origin point of the pastime that has come closer than almost anything to pulling me out of drug addiction. The equipment the fighters use is stuff that, if you were in the States and holding a garage sale, you wouldn't even put it out for sale. You'd simply throw it away. In Bangkok, it's what the professionals use.

At noontime and when the training days end, we wait in chow line and hold plates for the headmistress to spoon rice with bits of chicken from a heavy steel pot. When the rice is served with pork, Omar refuses; he is Muslim. We do not discuss religion, or politics. Along with the two Craig David hip-hop tunes and Ralph Lauren clothes, he has other Western tastes. He says "bee-atch" for *bitch* and knows the meanings of the words *extortionist* and *mafia*. He shows us how to take buses instead of spending money on taxis and how to haggle with vendors at open-air markets over knockoff American designer labels. I buy Ralph Lauren button-downs, and a t-shirt that says "Marijuana" made to look the logo of McDonald's.

A few days later, Caesar shows around a photograph he's taken.

"You look like a terrorist," someone tells Omar, commenting on the expression he wears in the picture.

"A terrorist? What is this?" Omar stares.

"A terrorist?" He repeats.

In December 2000, there's little reason to suspect—even if Omar only *pretended* not to know what "terrorist" meant—it is anything more than a reaction to the stereotype of "terrorist" attached to a young Muslim man of Middle Eastern descent.

Our week in Muay Thai camp ends. Cheetah and the rest of our California group return from Chiang Mai. Next stop, Pattaya Beach. I ask Cheetah to bring Omar along; Omar and I share a hotel room. We visit a tattoo artist he knows, who inks a dragon on the shoulder opposite my Hunter S. Thompson artwork. Unfortunately, the dragon turns out very

Six: Bangkok

phallic looking. Years later, a Norteño friend of mine with a tattoo gun will transform it into a fish-creature. He'll tattoo me in the dormitory of drug rehab, while we're both residents there.

After a few days in Pattaya Beach, we take the tour van back to Bangkok. Omar and I say our goodbyes in the lobby of Karnmanee Palace Hotel.

My time with Omar is a turning point. I could be like him, living in a foreign land. Borrow money from my parents. A few thousand dollars; it wouldn't take much. Spend a year in Thailand. Drug-free, living and training at the International Muay Thai Academy. It's highly unlikely I would ever fight in the stadiums, but I could write a book about the experience. About adventure, finding a way out of drugs.

Instead I'll go on to have a much different kind of adventure…

To live a unique sort of nightmare…

Omar, or at least a version of him, will be involved.

Omar will haunt my waking dreams as my addiction and mental states worsen. He will represent a quest, a journey through madness, to some new form of sanity…

To achieving my dream, even.

Still, too many times in the years to come my mind will drift and be shoved towards thoughts of the International Muay Thai Academy.

In my memories, I'm making the run.

From the wide boulevard with the crowed sidewalks, I follow Omar.

We are inches from speeding traffic, seconds from hunks of steel and churning fuel.

"A terrorist? What is this?"

Omar runs ahead of me. Every so often he looks back over his shoulder and motions for me to keep up, keep up. I have to follow him, or risk becoming hopelessly lost in the tangled streets.

Seven:
Home on Monterey Boulevard

The rich man builds a house, but the wise man builds a tomb.

—Carmina Epigraphica

The wheels on my plane from Bangkok drift just above the San Francisco runway. Thoughts of getting high are stronger than gravity's pull. There's only one way I know how to make those thoughts go away.

I go straight from the airport to score meth.

I fail to show up for work the Biotech Giant the next day.

Meth becomes an everyday thing. Four o'clock, bolt from my cubicle to the drug dealer's for my regular "Slappy Meal." Twenty bucks' worth of weed, forty worth of meth. Home to lock myself in my bedroom, get high, and pluck at an old Fender guitar. Masturbate.

There's one attempt at a return to Muay Thai. An hour or so of half-hearted flailing at Fairtex, before lying crumpled in the corner of the ring after a misaimed kick and a twisted knee.

Omar emails me at my Biotech Giant address. He calls me his brother; says he's getting ready to fight in the stadiums. There are a few words of what look like Arabic in the message.

I'll never hear from him again.

One September Tuesday morning, I wake to "Drops of Jupiter" playing on the radio. The deejay cries, reporting the news. I remember a documentary about a plane flying into the Empire State Building. Sometime that day or week, I write the FBI via their website. There's not much to tell them about my friend from Bangkok. I build a fantasy: Me, along with Omar, aboard one of those planes, overpowering the hijackers. Saving countless lives. Other Americans are at Ground Zero, saving lives.

My parents give me a loan for a down payment on a house. I fly to Massachusetts. I've been using speed and smoking weed every day for almost a year. My dad and I load his Jeep Cherokee full of furniture and belongings from my childhood home. A chest of drawers. The guitar he'd play sitting on the edge of my bed, singing songs before I went to sleep. The antique Regulator A pendulum clock that hung in the living room.

I'm at the round wooden kitchen table, eating a slice of pie my mother baked that afternoon.

"I can't believe it." My dad shakes his head as he comes in from the screen porch.

"What happened?" I put down my fork.

"I backed the Jeep into the apple tree. There's dent in the frame." It's uncharacteristic…my dad is careful, meticulous. "Remember you used to climb that tree?"

"I used to pretend it was a helicopter." The tree had a crook for a cockpit; I'd fly countless missions. My father goes upstairs to his office and returns with Jeep's title, signs it over to me.

I pick up Mark Burnsen. Our first gas stop as we head west, I buy an American flag sticker for the Cherokee's rear window. As we drive cross-country, it's possible Mark and I follow part of Jack Kerouac's route, the one his alter-ego Sal Paradise took crisscrossing the country in *On the Road*. Dean Moriarty—based on real person Neal Cassady—was Kerouac/Paradise's copilot.

"Between the dent and the flag, you can spot this thing in a parking lot no problem," Mark says from the Jeep's driver's seat. "We can make Niagara Falls before dark."

"Then there's the rock n' roll hall of fame, right?"

"Tomorrow." He nods, stomps the accelerator.

Delays are unavoidable. We don't make Niagara Falls until past nightfall, parking in the visitor lot and listening to the crush of water. After a night in a motel, we make Cleveland on a picture-perfect summer's day. The grounds of the Case Western Reserve University like a postcard. Later we wander the Hall of Fame.

"All the jokes about Cleveland," Mark says as we pass a glass case with Jimi Hendrix memorabilia. "It's beautiful here."

"It's really something," I say, trying to remember how old Jimi was when he died. The same age as Janis Joplin, Jim Morrison.

We push west. The Nebraska sky is a crossword-puzzle-grid of jet trails. "A month ago, you looked up, there was only blue sky," I say. "Everything was grounded." The Nebraska plains stretch before us two strangers to the land, headed to the storied West Coast.

Riding shotgun next to Mark Burnsen, a month or so after September 11th? Like Kerouac morphing into Sal Paradise, I start to sink into the mind-fog. Odd ideas come. I start dwelling on the dent in the Jeep...my otherwise careful and meticulous father backing into the apple tree. *Was it really an accident?*

The flag decal, in memory of the victims of 9/11.

I remember what Mark said—how the Jeep is easy to spot in a parking lot.

It would also be easy to spot for someone following us.

Dark thoughts grip me as the empty plains sweep past. I imagine what it might be like to hear the radio announcer describe a crime involving a child victim. The heinous act discovered at the diner where Mark and I ate our lunch an hour before. I picture us turning back the Jeep to assist the authorities. But finding suspicion cast upon us, until the real criminals are found. If they are found.

As darkness settles over the interstate-split near the Nebraska/Colorado border, Mark pilots the Jeep south, towards Denver. Last presumed home of Dean Moriarty's father, who disappeared into what might be modern-day soup kitchens and homeless shelters. In *On the Road*, Moriarty and Paradise search Denver to find him, but fail.

Mark and I ride around the city, looking for a music store and strings for my father's guitar. We don't find one. A few days later, we make San Francisco after dark. I take the wheel from Mark and drive past my apartment, out to Ocean Beach. I park facing the Pacific.

"We can't go any further," I tell him. "This is where America ends." A line from *Los Angeles Without a Map*, Richard Rayner's book about moving to LA from England, fashioning a new life within the strangeness. I read it back in college and always assumed it was a memoir, but it could've just as easily been fiction. Far in the distance a container vessel crawls towards land, its lights like fireflies in the Ashburnham fields.

Back at my apartment, I make up the couch for Mark. "I'm gonna go out for a few minutes. Then we can watch a movie or something." But my drug dealer's moved to a new part of town. By the time I've found his house and scored and returned home, Mark is asleep. In the morning I drive him to the airport. He has to be at work the next day.

The first close encounter with the San Francisco Police Department seems entirely outside my control. But I never would've let it happen, were it not for the meth.

I'm still living in my apartment, waiting for escrow to close on the house. It's two, three o'clock in the morning. I've been up partying when the doorbell rings.

Multiple times, insistent.

Naked, I throw on my terry-cloth bathrobe. A gift from Poem I'd kept through the years. I peek out the window. Parked blocking the driveway, a squad car. The headlights like eyes peering into the fog.

"We had a call," the officer tells me, through the bars of my front-door gate. "Domestic violence."

A couple weeks before, I'd let one of my meth friends jerry-rig a telephone line in my apartment. Something must've happened; the wires crossed.

"There's no one here but me," I tell him.

"I'm gonna have to take a look around." The cop is a young guy, in good shape. Working on his own; no backup. Strange…

supposedly most police officer injuries occur in domestic violence incidents. I let him in because I'm high and—by his account—there's a domestic violence situation happening *somewhere*. The police just got the wrong address. I figure he'll come inside for a quick look, and go help the victim, wherever she is.

He performs a thorough search, by the book. Opens closet doors, inspect the back steps, shines his flashlight under my bed.

At one point he spots the Fairtex poster on my wall in red, white, blue.

"You work out at Fairtex?" he asks.

"I used to." I adjust the belt on my bathrobe.

He turns to my bookshelves. My paperback collection and various knickknacks accumulated through the years. The clay bier stein from German festival. Something else, too. A bag of marijuana; big, fat green buds. I've forgotten to hide them.

"You've been smoking weed," he says. "At least I know you're not violent."

It's never made clear what happened, whether the victim of domestic violence got help. That interaction, with single officer familiar with Fairtex and sympathetic to my marijuana habit, keeps the psychic wheels turning. Police are becoming a familiar presence in my life.

New Year's Eve. Escrow closed, I'm in the process of moving into the home at 241 Monterey Boulevard. Maia's come home with me. I'm showing her around the place.

"Reverse mitosis," I say. "I'm gonna turn it all into one big place."

Seven: Home on Monterey Boulevard

"People lived here?" Maia takes off her jacket, looks for somewhere to put it among the cardboard moving boxes.

"It was two apartments." I take her jacket and set it down near the Regulator A clock leaning against a wall. "I've got two of everything. Kitchens, bathrooms, living rooms…"

"You'll live here by yourself?"

"I've always wanted a puppy."

Beyond the picture window, the expanse of the Excelsior District. The home is high up on a hill, three glorious stories rising above Monterey Boulevard.

"Maybe…maybe I'll get the place painted."

"You could paint it yourself. It's not that hard." Maia twists a strand of hair, stops herself, grins, and looks for a cigarette.

"I don't know…hey, you want a line?" The meth is stashed inside the Regulator A, near where the pendulum arm connects. I pour some shards onto a CD case—*Exile on Main Street,* the Stones' double album—and chop it with an expired credit card.

"No, thanks." She moves around the kitchen. One of the kitchens. "You could do a lot. Get rid of the linoleum, new appliances."

"I know contractors." I'm thinking of meth connections who work in the trades.

"Yeah. But you could do a lot yourself, too." She tries to light her cigarette, but her lighter keeps throwing out sparks. I find her some matches, roll up a twenty, and snort a line. It burns my nostrils, and I pinch the bridge of my nose, waiting for the pain to subside.

"Got anything to drink?"

I open a bottle of wine and pour two glasses. "Have you resolved anything?" I say.

"What?"

"You know…New Year's. Or resolved not to do anything?"

"Oh. No. I always feel like I'm cheating myself." She holds her glass up to the light and looks at it a long time. "Making some promise like that." She rummages through the cardboard boxes, picks up a black-and-white photograph. A soldier, epaulets hanging off his uniform.

"It's from the Revolutionary War."

"No," she says. "No photographs back then. He looks like you."

"Some relative, I guess."

"He looks just like you. Hey, nice watch," she says, noticing my Rolex.

"My father gave it to me. They're gonna bury me with it."

We embrace, begin undressing one another. We're on the air mattress…I'm getting paranoid. Peeking through the blinds. A white van marked with the logo for Tommantino's Poultry Company slow cruises along Monterey, down the hill.

"What are they, working? Not on New Year's Eve," I say.

"It's New Year's *Day*," she says. "Now it is. It's cold. Do you have a t-shirt?"

I want to rise from the air mattress.

"What's the matter? What's out there?"

"I don't know," I say. "Nothing, maybe."

I peer out at the New Year, now arrived. Find the t-shirt with the McDonald's marijuana logo from Bangkok. Wishing she'd change her mind. For some reason, I think about a scene

Seven: Home on Monterey Boulevard

from the book *The Basketball Diaries*—author Jim Carroll, descending into heroin addiction, agonizes over his desire for a woman he can't be with. Until he realizes the woman he *is* with, is her twin sister.

I put my arm around Maia, wanting to sleep.

I wake in the Jeep's passenger seat, parked in the Biotech Giant employee lot. A Beatles song plays. I glance at my Rolex—wondering if my manager is wondering when I'll return from lunch. *If I'll return.* That morning, my manager had asked me to her office for a heart-to-heart talk.

"This is terrible," I'd said. Brenda's computer monitor showed internet news of post-September 11th.

"It's a different world," she said. Her eyes teared up. Mine did too. Silence, then: "You were doing a good job." Brenda's monitor went dark as she spoke. Next to it, a photograph of her with her husband on a vacation, a mountain's dual peaks behind them, red desert sand under their feet.

"What do you think the problem is?" I'm trying to get a sense of how much she suspects about the drugs.

"I don't know," she says. "I don't know."

Later, I'm on my daily long walk around the Giant's campus. There's a bench, down steps and out-of-view of office windows. One can sit and smoke; watch airplanes take off and land at the twin runways of San Francisco International Airport.

I find my way to my Jeep, fall asleep in the driver's seat.

The Beatles tune ends, and a John Lennon song starts, something off *Double Fantasy*. Lunchtime deejay special, twofer Tuesdays. I pull a lever; the driver's seat raises upright. There's a little mirror clipped behind the sun visor, and I cut a line, roll up a twenty-dollar bill.

The sound of squealing tires, like the cops rolling in. But it's just my co-workers parking. I duck as they walk past, carrying to-go bags from the local Italian restaurant. Smiling and laughing. They'd invited me to lunch. I couldn't imagine hovering over a half-eaten plate of gnocchi, trying to hide being high on drugs. There on the Jeep's floorboards, a boxer's hand-wrap from Thailand. It's rolled up, ready for use. I push it under the seat.

The next day, I'm smoking a cigarette behind the home on Monterey Boulevard when my cell phone rings. I figure it's someone from the Biotech Giant, and I'm right.

"Hello?" The voice says. "I'm calling from Human Resources. Brenda, your manager…um, your former manager…forwarded me the email you had sent."

A pause. The voice says: "You've decided to resign?"

A maple tree grows in the back yard. When the season is right, its leaves are the color of blood. The year I was born, my father planted a maple tree behind our house. A few feet from the apple tree/helicopter into which my dad backed his Jeep. Every summer we watched the maple tree outgrow me. It will remain tall and majestic in Ashburnham, a few feet from the Cellar Hole, long after I'm gone.

"Hello?" the voice says. "Are you there?"

The sun goes behind a cloud, and I'm trying to find air.

"So, you've decided to resign." No longer a question.

"I decided," I manage, "to fix up my house."

"I see."

Seven: Home on Monterey Boulevard

"It's a full-time job."

"Yes. Well, there's the matter of your company credit card."

The last time I'd used the card was at a strip club in Montreal on a business trip. By coincidence, Uncle Jupiter had been in Montreal at the same time. We'd met for lunch (not at the strip club). My cigarette smoke drifts upwards. A plane climbs into its flight path, engines beating back gravity, wings' curvature forcing air, generating lift.

"Well," the HR person says after I've told her where in my desk—*my former desk*—to find the credit card, "we can certainly appreciate your contributions."

The plane forces its ascent, and when it's perpendicular to me, directly above, pulls into a steep angle. As if it became lighter, dropping a payload…*a bomb, maybe*…or a pallet of food/medicine hooked to a parachute. Whatever the Perpendicular Plane might've dropped would've landed right on top of me.

"There's some final documentation," the HR person tells me. I realize she's a friendly sort, just doing her job. Which, as soon as the call ends, will no longer involve me. "Do you have a personal email?"

"I'm not really connected that way…"

"If you can provide a physical address, we'll make certain everything gets to you."

The Perpendicular Plane's engine-whine fades until no longer audible. There's a pause, until she says: "Just out of curiosity, what's it like to fix up a home?"

"You need companionship."

"Really?"

"Yes," I say. "It's why I think I'll adopt a puppy."

Eight:
Mickey

In establishing contact with strange people Charley* is my ambassador. I release him, and he drifts towards the objective...(a) child can do the same thing, but a dog is better.

—John Steinbeck, *Travels with Charley*
*Steinbeck's poodle

A blur of fur; black, gray, and white... tail wagging, toenails scrabbling, tongue flapping like a medieval banner...he races across the pet store linoleum like he'll run right out of his feet. I'm squatting, arms thrown open.

He mad rushes, leaps...

And bites me on the nose.

The bite is superficial. No bleeding or scars. *Does he somehow know I snort speed? Is he trying to tell me something?*

I'll come to believe further in this particular dog's supernatural powers.

I don't much care for his name, Nikki. Yet I hate to change it; at three months old, he's getting used to it. But, *Mickey*... not too much different.

In the days and years to come, Mickey will prove nothing short of a miracle. A hyper-animated sprite in a wolf-dog's

Eight: Mickey

body. He teaches himself tricks: how to dance backwards, mimic cats, position himself between the Earth and the low-hanging full moon on our midnight walks atop San Francisco's rocky hills; his silhouette that of a coyote spirit guide. Mickey is a dog you stop to take a second look at... white fur on his feet like athletic socks, wolfish countenance, long, thick fangs. A range of facial expressions would put TV commercial actors to shame. They say the more primitive looking a dog, the smarter.

Such is the case with Mickey.

I don't spend any more time, effort, or money on Mickey than you'd spend on your average newborn. An entire wing of my library is dedicated to dog-raising books. I cook him brown rice and chicken to stave off diarrhea. He has more chew toys than a preschool has art supplies. A corner of the home on Monterey Boulevard becomes a grooming-and-nail-clipping space, after he's had his weekly bath in the galvanized-steel tub set up in a sunny corner of the yard.

Mornings, Mickey and I ride in the Jeep to the dog park. Me sipping from a giant Peet's coffee with *plenty sugar* (with the meth, you love the sugar). Mickey, with his head near the window, catching a million scents.

Mickey was a stray, found wandering the graveyard with his littermates. Never properly socialized. At the dog park, he raises his hackles and tucks his tail between his legs when other canines approach.

Scared and mistrustful of his own kind…

Yet soon enough he's leaping and running and batting the air with his forepaws, joyful in his place among the other dogs. I love watching him run, play, learn to be himself.

"Cool dog!" a smiling young man calls from a passing car, giving the thumbs-up as I walk Mickey along Monterey Boulevard.

The more time spent with Mickey, the less I see my friends and family. I don't know how they might be reacting. Solitude equals safety. Mostly I only resent human beings around me, anyway. *Nothing or no one good enough to suit me.* In February 2003, a year after quitting the Biotech Giant, I haven't thought much about writing. Haven't thought much about anything, really, except doing meth, raising Mickey…turning our home on Monterey Boulevard into a palace.

Many nights our Jeep Cherokee drifts along the 280 freeway, my meth-hands unsteady at the wheel, arriving at the Home Depot parking lot thirty minutes before midnight closing time. I've got my coffee with *plenty sugar* swilled to the dregs,

Eight: Mickey

Marlboro dangling from my lips. Mickey strains against his leash as I let him poke through the hillside vegetation alongside the parking lot. Sometimes I'll bring him into the Home Depot with me. We walk the aisles like a newlywed couple scanning for items for our starter home.

An hour or so later, back on Monterey Boulevard, Mickey rests on his cedar-filled bed, gnawing a marrow bone just the way he likes it. Its center filled with peanut butter and frozen solid in my stainless-steel freezer. The freezer matches the stove, which matches the Israeli sink. With the Jeep backed into the garage alongside my BMW bike, I unload bag after bag of Home Depot merchandise. It goes with the rest of the tools assembled in the garage: circular saw, chop saw, handsaw, reciprocating saw…anything the Home Depot sells with metal bladed teeth. All manner of hammers, drills, screwdrivers, paintbrushes, work lights…a shop-vac, a tool belt. And the materials: buckets of drywall mud, armloads of lumber remnants, boxes of nails…

Didn't you once read about settlers on the American plains? They burned down their homes when they moved, to salvage the nails.

I'm listening to Brenda, my old manager from the Biotech Giant. I'm letting her talk to me in my mind. I've invented a game where she follows me around, comments thoughtfully, makes helpful, firm suggestions on how I might improve. I don't hear her voice outside of my head.

You know, the Biotech Giant has employee assistance. We would've helped you get into treatment, get well again.

Afternoons I'll landscape the back yard, planting flowers on the hillside. Mickey, the magnificent beast, tears around after his tennis ball, works at his marrow bone, sleeps in the sun. I heft pick and shovel; careful, so as not to break the antique bottles I find buried. The bottles are like those my father found in the Cellar Hole. In the old days, the Lane family in Ashburnham—and whoever lived at Monterey Boulevard, long before me—threw their trash outside. Most of it decomposed or was eaten by animals. But the bottles remained. My father washed them, set them on the windowsills to glint in the sun, colored glass remnants from a long-gone place. I do the same with the bottles I find.

I graduate from snorting meth to smoking it. As day turns to dusk, I'm in a garage with my meth people. A bare bulb struggles to throw cold light and dispel shadows on the stone wall. A door opens, and Rich step-hops over an oil stain on the cement floor, almost landing his boot on Mickey's forepaw. Rich is a drug dealer's drug dealer. The first one to fill the pipe, the guy who when your doorbell rings, you want him to be the one ringing it. Strippers hang out with him on their nights off.

The meth pipe gets passed around our ragged circle. When it gets handed to me, instead of quickly passing it to my left, I ask Rich how to smoke.

"You want to exhale quickly," he says. "It ain't like pot smoke. Hold it in too long, your lungs might explode." I like the taste of the meth smoke…sort of a sweet stickiness…and the feeling. No more of that terrible nasal burn and ammonia drip in the back of the throat.

I like sitting alone downstairs in the home on Monterey Boulevard, rocked back in my black leather armchair….

Eight: Mickey

Cradling my meth pipe, smoking at leisure, drawing hits again and again.

It feels like I could go this way until I die.

I write a song I call "Peeled Ears."

It's past midnight
So you better keep your ears peeled
A voice from a dream whispers your name
And tells you how you feel
Don't make a sound
Try not even to breathe
Just a dose of that special potion, baby, that's all you need
Floating through a lake of clear fire
Made by the melting snow
A clear glass globe gently bathed in a pale-blue glow
Who'll come knocking, when the door is locked up tight?

I write of the lake of clear fire that is meth crystals liquefied by pale-blue flame from the propane torch, in the pipe's clear glass globe. I sit with the paranoia that tends to ensue.

I'm noticing things in the night skies. A meteorite blazes a green trail as I swerve the Jeep through the Miraloma District switchbacks. Sticks of lighting poke from the inky blackness above the airport, the sky visible from my cigarette perch behind my home on Monterey Boulevard. Bats flap above the backyard. Multiple helicopters circle over my house. More and more Perpendicular Planes, passing *directly overhead*…too many for coincidence!

A strange spotlight shines on me as I sit at my round teakwood dining table, in one of the four matching chairs.

Purchased from Papenhousen on West Portal, down the street from Uncle Jupiter's. Eating my 10:00 p.m. breakfast—standard fare for your handyman meth smoker whose personal rule is never to begin painting the walls until after midnight. The spotlight shines from beyond the bay windows. From the streets of the Excelsior District, pointed up at a shallow angle.

The spotlight shines on me…

One of your central concerns about psychosis. I *am seeing* these things, just like I *will hear* the Boolean Operators, soon enough. What I see in the night skies *cannot be* hallucinations. Later, when the psychosis takes hold, my mind will decide the voices cannot be hallucinations, either. The psychosis hijacks the mind…compels the mind to notice what must be real, then causes the mind, under duress, to invent explanations for why what isn't real, must be.

An article appears in the March 23, 2003 *New York Times Magazine* (the cover story is "Al Qaeda's Philosopher"). The article describes HyperSonic Sound. Invented by Woody Norris, it gives anyone the power to project sound that "feels like it's inside your skull" to a person who has no idea from where the sound is coming. I read it sitting at the round teakwood table as the spotlight shines from the Excelsior District.

Mickey leaves his marrow bone, saunters over to let me rub his prehistoric head. The brain inside like the one that led pack-mates to the hunt, out of starvation, little more than instinct as guide. I think of my meth pipe, of tramping downstairs to ride out the night. My home on Monterey Boulevard rises quietly in the darkness. In the bottom floor, sitting in my black leather armchair, the meth melts in the glass globe

Eight: Mickey

as I work the blue propane flame, a blob of heat held steadier than death's approach. My armchair is reclined into oblivion. Mickey, the coyote spirit guide upstairs, guarding our home. Pattering paw-falls on the ceiling/floor above. I, drawing from my pipe again and again, am little more than beast-human.

I page through Phyllis Balch's *Prescription for Nutritional Healing*. Searching for my symptoms, what their causes might be. Adrenal Disorder, candidiasis, environmental toxicity, hypothyroidism, kidney disease, schizophrenia, weakened immune system…hoping to discover the reason my health is decaying is due to a source identifiable within the pages of a book. Something treatable with herbal remedy.

In the days to come, I begin noticing fake newspaper stories.

Somehow the *San Francisco Chronicle* has begun appearing on my doorstop. The grayish newsprint pages contain an article on the outcome of a boxing match. But on the facing page, an ad for that same match—it isn't scheduled to take place until the following Saturday! Another story seems to be no more than gibberish, something about Robin Williams going on a yachting race with Larry Ellison.

A few nights later, I recline in my black leather armchair, smoking from my glass pipe. I start hearing a buzzing sound. *Coming from inside my head*. The buzzing dials in until it becomes a radio sportscaster, doing play-by-play of a ballgame. The words are impossible to make out, but there's the unmistakable sportscaster's rhythm and cadence.

Not a problem, I think. *It's just my tooth fillings, picking up radio broadcasts.*

Sure. That happens.

The police interactions, the strange things in the night skies, the auditory hallucinations for which I come up with rational-seeming explanations…on the surface I'm too gone on meth to deal with it.

Yet the fear and rage boil underneath. Too much pressure, until I start taking it out on the living being I cherish most.

"Hey! You shouldn't treat a dog like that!" The woman is yelling from her car. She's pulled over to police me. Maybe report animal abuse. I'm shaking Mickey by the scruff, in retribution for some perceived slight. Terrified—if he doesn't listen to me, something horrible will happen.

We had a dog when I was a kid. Lockett was a collie mix. One summer leafy-green evening, the Ashburnham air fragrant with flowers, Blossom and I and some of the neighborhood kids rode our bicycles along a dirt driveway. I, being the oldest, was in the lead. Lockett ran a few feet ahead of me. She trotted into the road, not knowing to stop and look both ways.

The car never had a chance to slow down. Blossom and I screamed, racing up our sledding-hill to our parents. The poor driver…imagine going for a summer's drive, maybe to your buddy's for a couple beers, and you mash some kids' dog into the pavement, have to hear them scream at the top of their lungs.

Mickey trots towards the woman, tongue out, tail wagging. "You shouldn't treat a dog like that." She's not as angry. "People can see you, you know." Now Mickey's got his front paws up on the driver door, letting her scratch his ears.

"He's a good dog," she says. "People can see you, you know."

Eight: Mickey

Difficult, to write about a person who mistreats an innocent dog. Especially when that person is *me*. Powerful individuals and things are coming after me. Or so psychosis forces my hijacked mind to believe. I, in turn, go after Mickey. Terrified if he doesn't learn to listen to me, he'll end up like Lockett.

I shake his snout near the mess he made on the living room floor. Forget to feed him, too high on meth. Swat him with a rolled-up newspaper for seeming to bare his teeth at me. I do it all, and more.

To be fair, little I do is what you'd call horrific. Most of what went on between Mickey and me was the usual dog-owner love and companionship. Were I to give myself the benefit of perspective? If you add up all the times I mistreated Mickey during the years we were together, it probably wouldn't stack up to a week's worth of the suffering your typical livestock animal endures, raised for slaughter on the modern farm. Still, you wouldn't have to be any special sort of animal lover to hate me for the times I mistreated Mickey.

A weird thing happens once I get clean, years later. Obsessions set in. Food obsessions…constant thoughts about calories, types of nutrients, food's effect on the metabolism. Sleep obsessions…always worried whether I'll get enough. Obsessions over running, the exercise I'll keep coming back to. I have physical problems. My skin is flakey, like I have dandruff on my arms and trunk. And I for a long time I'll compulsively scratch my skin.

It won't be until I'm years away from meth I'll realize: Food, sleep, and running? *These are the same things a dog obsesses over.* Skin dandruff? Like a dog shedding. Scratching? I might as well scratch my face with my foot, like a dog with a hind leg.

You may be saying I should hate myself for how I treated Mickey. There's been enough of that, believe me. Mickey, in some fashion, reaches to me from across the spirit world…hence my obsessions. Now Mickey—or whatever he represents—trains me to bring some measure of good to my surroundings.

But that won't come until much later.

In 2003, I'll be haunted by a presence that, at the time, I choose to see as little less than sinister.

The Boolean Operators arrive in force.

Nine:
The Boolean Operators

> ...*the types of delusions that Nash* suffered from are particularly characteristic of...paranoid schizophrenia... both grandiose and persecutory, often shifting from one to the other in the space of moments or even including both at the same time...although all were organized, in subtle ways, around coherent themes.*
>
> —Sylvia Nasar, *A Beautiful Mind*
> *John Nash, Nobel Prize winner, mathematics

I'm in my garage, high on meth and marijuana. Us San Francisco meth people, we love garages. I suck clean the Jeep's interior with an industrial vacuum. Having spent the afternoon carting off waste from a garden project. Maple tree clippings and flower petals lined rugged burlap bundles I trucked off to the dump.

The Sunnyside Conservatory stands directly across Monterey Boulevard. A decrepit version of the old-time bandstands we'd see in the New England town squares when my parents drove around antique shopping. Blossom and I in the back seat, playing with our stuffed animals. Making the animals talk, giving them unique voices. They'd comment on the scenery and, of course, throw the occasional barb at our father behind the wheel.

I read somewhere one of the first patriarchs to settle the Monterey Boulevard area had Sunnyside Conservatory built on his estate. But for years it was lost in the forest, badly in need of repair. Missing windows; tagged with graffiti. Long after Mickey and I are gone, a local community group will restore it to glory. It will become a popular spot for weddings.

A woman strolls past as I work the nozzle. Brown hair, jeans, a light-blue sweatshirt with a logo for Pacific Surf Construction. Her walk, her body type—she could be an Olympic downhiller, a hurdler.

"Hi," I say.

"Hello." She smiles.

I glance after her. Somehow, she transforms into a fourteen-year-old girl, skipping past the neighbor's gate.

No…that can't be right…

Too much meth, marijuana.

But like those thoughts from the Nebraska plains, it seems real.

Never mind. I return to the Jeep. Moments later, she's back. Now in her original form, a grown woman. "I just had to tell you," she says, "you're an attractive man."

This is Kim S.

With her statement, she may be the only person in this book more disturbed than I.

At first, I think it's a joke. Someone watching me on camera, hidden in the bramble of the Sunnyside Conservatory.

"Thanks," I say, embarrassed. "Where are you headed?"

Nine: The Boolean Operators

"I'm going to get my ya-yas out." I don't know what it's supposed to mean. Other than it's the title of a Stones' album. "Then to class," she says. "Nursing school."

"Oh, yeah? My mom's a nurse. My sister, too."

A white van cruises past: Tommantino's Poultry Company. The van's been appearing more regularly...it followed me to the top of Market Street, after a 3:00 a.m. Safeway run.

"Do you like dogs?" I ask her. For some reason Mickey's in the house. Sleeping, maybe, or having at a marrow bone.

"Well," she says, "no. Not really." Kim S. leans against the washing machine. The metal door is like Natalie LaFontane's locker in the Oakmont hallway. On the shelf above her, there's the milk crate with my boxing gloves and shinguards.

"Can I have your phone number?" I blurt it out, before there's the chance to make a mistake.

My cell phone rings that afternoon. I sit at the round teakwood table.

"Where did you grow up?" Kim asks.

"Massachusetts. I was your stereotype kid—had to get out of the small town; move to the big city."

"I live in Pacifica," she says. "Hey, do you know Dave Grohl?"

"Sure," I say. "I know who he is. The musician."

"He's my brother-in-law. I'm driving to San Diego to see him in concert."

I think about Poem...she was from San Diego. And it strikes me Kim *seems to have adopted a Boston accent.*

"What do you do?" Kim asks.

I tell her about the Biotech Giant. "But I always wanted to

remodel a home. You gotta have goals."

"I hear you," she says.

We decide to meet for coffee when she returns from San Diego. Later that evening, as the sun sinks below the Sunnyside Conservatory, I sit in the backyard. As I stroke Mickey's fur and spray the flower garden with a hose, I hear the first of the voices.

From the other side of the house, a ghostly female voice…

The voice calls my name.

It is the voice of my grandmother, long since dead.

Or my aunt Koral, Jupiter's wife.

If you've ever seen the Clint Eastwood movie *Pale Rider*, where his character the Preacher hears his name called across the dusty, shimmering California plain? The voice calling my name sounds so real, I have to force myself not to go and check to see if someone's there. I water the flowers, their roots maybe wrapped around colored glass bottles still unearthed.

The voice calls my name. She says nothing else.

The coming days bring a different type of disembodied voices…

I hear victims in trouble. Their arguments and pleas for help, drifting across the afternoon air, passing through the open window as I sit smoking my meth pipe in my black leather armchair. A man sobs after his girlfriend accidentally shot himself with his pistol. A woman and her father are locked into a screaming match. She was the victim of rape. He blames her—for the clothes she wore on her date.

I shouldn't be hearing voices like this.

I shouldn't hear the sportscaster buzzing in my tooth fillings…

Just after midnight on the day after Passover begins, I'm reclined in my black leather armchair. Smoking from my pipe.

Nine: The Boolean Operators

From behind the southeast wall, my father starts talking to me.

"SON," his disembodied voice says, "GET ON THE BUS!"

A vision comes...a yellow school bus rolling to a stop.

"GET ON THE BUS, SON!"

My first-ever day of school, my father waited with me at the bus stop, a few feet from the Cellar Hole. The bus rolled along the country road, under a canopy of green leaves, rolling over the same spot where Lockett took her last steps. I leapt aboard, afraid it might leave without me. It was the same bus I'd cry on, when the driver pulled over until the rowdy kids settled down.

"GET ON THE BUS, SON!"

The Boolean Operators have come for me.

There's no mistaking them now.

Methamphetamine psychosis. I've bought the ticket; now I'm on the ride.

It doesn't occur to me to fight the current...when my Boolean dad talks to me from behind the walls, *I am comfortable accepting where I am.* Even if I'm not happy there.

Methamphetamine psychosis.

Imagine being locked in an attic. Musty, dark except for a low-wattage bare bulb. Splintery rafters, wooden planks with nailheads jutting up from the dusty floor. Cobwebs caress your skin; dust chokes your lungs. The attic is filled with old comic books. Teetering stacks everywhere, with faded inks and yellowed newsprint. You gingerly lift a comic from the top of a stack, brush grime from the cover, run a finger-pad over a coarse rusty staple.

You begin turning the pages.

Images and words meet you. Super-powered heroes,

grotesque villains, fantastic landscapes, futuristic planets.

You choose other comic books, begin flipping to random pages. More words and images...

Soon you are no longer reading the words in those dialogue/thought bubbles.

You *hear them*. The same as you hear actors on TV.

Instead of seeing the comics on the page, they are *visions in your mind*.

You can't escape the attic; the door remains shut tight against a rusty iron hasp...

You are *in the comic books*.

You are praised as a hero; you become outraged as a victim... others blame you as the villain. The scenes degenerate deeper into horrific. The characters are *people you know*—they are tortured, maimed, butchered. Your family members have committed terrible crimes—murder, treason, extortion—and are desperate to *set you up* to take the blame.

You are trapped in the attic with the comic books...

And the attic is your mind.

Methamphetamine psychosis.

It's not clear how the Boolean Operators got their name. Perhaps because "Operator" sounds a little like "Doppelgänger," and a definition of "Boolean" is, "a binary variable, having two possible values called 'true' and 'false.'"

Boolean Operators have no material form. They can't understand things like pain, death, or trauma. A Boolean will "suicide" itself or another Boolean as a way of expressing melancholy. Or it will "torture to death" another Boolean as a way to show

Nine: The Boolean Operators

mild annoyance. Acts of treason resulting in the fiery deaths of thousands are a Boolean's way of expressing resentment.

Boolean Operators often sound like real people—those I know, or public figures. A real person might be "Uncle Jupiter" or "Robert S. Mueller, Director of the FBI." Their disembodied voice versions are "Boolean Uncle Jupiter" or "Boolean Bob Mueller."

The Boolean Operators are at their worst as my Boolean Uncle Jupiter. He follows me everywhere, spewing mocking insults. He has architected grand and terrible conspiracies, with dire consequences for me.

"I IMPLANTED A GRAIN-OF-RICE TRANSPONDER IN YOUR NECK." Boolean Uncle Jupiter boasts of having stolen top-secret military technology. The grain-of-rice transponder allows my friends—all of whom Boolean Jupiter recruited to terrorize me—to talk to me from their "headquarters." A top-tier hotel suite rented by the San Francisco Police Department.

"THE POLICE ARE SPONSORING THIS ENTIRE OPERATION!" Boolean Uncle Jupiter shouts in triumph. "YOU SEE HOW BADLY YOUR METH HAS HURT US?"

"THE DEVICE HAS MALFUNCTIONED," Boolean Uncle Jupiter admits, his disembodied voice now tinged with regret. "YOU WILL SOON DIE." Indeed. The broken grain-of-rice transponder leaks toxins into my jugular (how someone could implant a transponder in my neck without me knowing, is a detail never made clear).

Enraged, frustrated, desperate, I leap from the black leather armchair or round teakwood table. Spin the Cherokee around

San Francisco. Mickey in the passenger's seat, wearing an expression of grave doubt. Sometimes I'll have to pull over, unable to breathe properly. Find a paper bag among the detritus scattered around the Jeep's floorboards. Put it to my face and huff plain air, until rebreathing my own carbon monoxide calms my heart and lungs.

"WE HAVE ORDERED A KIDNEY STRIKE!" Boolean Uncle Jupiter screams. My Peet's coffee with *plenty sugar* is hypnotically poisoned. The mind-dagger stabs pain into my kidney, I have to pull over and sprawl over the Jeep's hood, moaning for help until Boolean Jupiter calls off the strike.

"YOU MUST APPEAR HERE—WHERE WE ARE!" With Boolean Jupiter's words, it's back to the search. Boolean Operators directing me to the hotel suite where my friends are holed up with the rogue SFPD. I storm into the lobby, stare down the employees I believe are in on the conspiracy. Roam hallways of apartment buildings, knocking on random doors as the Boolean Operators give me apartment numbers.

Boolean Uncle Jupiter eludes me. He is a criminal, working with rogue elements of the San Francisco Police Department to frame me, send me to prison for life. He is a spy for the Mossad, having sold Army secrets from his position in Heidelberg. My mind is a host vehicle the psychosis-hijacker forces to hurtle towards catastrophe.

I'm in the emergency room. An MD specializing in psychiatric disorders is attending to me.

It happens to be the same day as Poem's birthday.

They'd sprung the intervention a couple hours ago.

Nine: The Boolean Operators

For a week or more I'd been ambushing my friends. Frantic talk of my house being bugged, stalkers cursing at me from passing motor scooters, the severed heads of dogs appearing lodged under the wheels of parked cars. I'd stood from the Passover Seder, hurled an excuse at Uncle Jupiter, and stormed out the door left ajar for the prophet Elijah. Escaped to my home to Monterey Boulevard to play tug-of-war with Mickey, smoke meth, and paint ceilings until three in the morning.

I'd had plans to meet friends at the Cafe Riggio on Geary Boulevard. A block or so from where Poem and I first met at Pat O'Sheas Mad Hatter. But when I arrived, something was wrong. Uncle Jupiter was there, along with a couple other friends from college.

"Why don't we take you to the emergency room?" somebody said.

It's how these things are done. Surprise—combined with superior numbers. Designed with psychology in mind. The hope of the interventionists is the intervened-upon will go along with whatever is suggested. It works, in my case. Half an hour later, I find myself in the UCSF emergency room.

Nobody tells me, "We are trying to have you committed to a psychiatric institution." Yet my hijacked mind decides this is what's happening. For years I allow myself the excuse: To seek help, to be honest about what I see and hear and believe, will lead to further attempts to have me committed.

USCF discharges me the same night. The attempt by my friends and family to have me committed has failed. Not only do I believe this to be reality; I see it as a victory.

It must have been hard on them. My Uncle Jupiter, especially.

Trained for decades by the Army to be responsible for the welfare of others. Now with his own nephew's closest friends coming to him, with stories of the nephew's mind deteriorating from drug abuse. Jupiter has had maybe had a sip of beer and two glasses of wine in his entire life. He must have felt compelled to do something. And not just anything. Something with the highest degree of certainty of fixing the problem. I don't mean to take an easy jab at the military when I say my Uncle Jupiter couldn't have felt it acceptable to lob a hand grenade at an enemy sniper's position when he had a phalanx of tanks at his disposal.

It must have been hard on my friends. I didn't wake up one day struck by meth psychosis, like one is struck by lightning. They'd known about my drug use for years. At some level they must have felt responsible. As if they should have seen it coming. My circle of friends must have felt they had no other choice go along with Uncle Jupiter's plan. Knowing in their hearts it was the best plan he knew how to come up with.

Even if they *were trying* to have me committed (and to this day, there's no proof they were), one must look past others' actions, to their intentions. If they'd staged the intervention differently? With women involved, in a home rather than an emergency room? It may have been no more successful. I would've been angry, hostile. Almost all the friends who were there that night are still my friends.

And, let's face it…if I'd never done meth, no one would ever have tried to have me committed.

Nine: The Boolean Operators

The day after my intervention, I call Kim S. "I'm sorry," I venture, unable to believe what I'm hearing myself say. "I can't meet you for coffee today. Last night, I went to the hospital." I take a deep breath and look at the southeast wall. "I've got, um…I've got a problem. Ah…substance abuse."

"I'm so proud of you!" I'm not sure she heard me right. "It takes a lot to admit that."

She tells me she can help. She drives her Mercedes up from Pacifica. We're drinking green tea, sitting across from one another at a coffee shop.

"So…how was San Diego, Dave Grohl's concert?"

"He brought me on stage! The crowd sung Happy Birthday." She wraps her hands around her cup, for warmth. "So, about your problem…"

It's funny, I think, *Kim's birthday is around the same time as Poem's.*

"Yeah. My family knows everything, I guess. I'm almost out of money, cashed in my retirement accounts. No job."

"Have you tried AA?"

"Once." A white van passes the window, slows for a yellow light.

"I know some people I can put you in touch with."

I stare at the van. Tommantino's.

Kim sips her tea, and I notice *the ring on her finger.* It's silver and inlaid with a wave pattern. Years ago, I'd worn the same ring. I'd had the wave pattern tattooed around my right bicep, then I'd given the ring to Blossom.

"A lot of people get clean. Get their jobs back, keep their homes."

"Sure," I say. I notice Kim's watch...*very similar to the Rolex my mom wears, which matches the Rolex my dad gave me...*

As Kim and I walk from the coffee shop, my mind creates a force field around us. Warding off negative energy, protecting us. "Look," she says, when we arrive at her red Mercedes, "I brought you something." She produces a small jade turtle. I put in in my pocket and wonder if I should try to kiss her. Decide I shouldn't.

Kim S. represents a chance for me to change. She gives me every reason to quit meth. Which is exactly what I do...

For a day or two.

Then, the addict's plan...I'll get high tonight, quit for good tomorrow.

I never take that first hit without fooling myself; *this time it will be different.*

It's like a horrible accident is about to happen and I can't tear my eyes away. *I'm* the accident. The more I thrash about in the vortex of addiction, the stronger it pulls me down. I *know* where it's all headed, but feel powerless to stop it. Spending one night clean, without meth, is so hard. And one night is like a grain of sand on a beach. Even if I make it to dawn, I'll just start using again tomorrow. Or the next day. Why postpone the inevitable?

How can one even *conceive* of a lifetime without drugs?

And, the part of me I can't yet connect with on the surface, understands...quitting meth, would force me to undertake a journey to become a writer. What if I got clean, pursued my dream, and failed? The pain of staying a meth addict is more bearable. The world of the Boolean Operators is one in which

Nine: The Boolean Operators

I feel I can survive.

Even triumph.

I'm walking Mickey and as I step from a curb, the jade turtle Kim S. gave me falls from my shirtfront pocket, shattering on the asphalt.

I begin tearing down my other worlds.

Nine-and-a-Half:
Theories

Gaslighting is a tactic in which a person or entity, in order to gain more power, makes a victim question their reality... (a)nyone is susceptible to gaslighting, and it is a common technique of abusers, dictators, "narcissists," and cult leaders.

—Stephanie A. Sarkis Ph.D.,
Psychology Today, January 22, 2017

I rip the home on Monterey Boulevard to pieces. Smash holes through the sheetrock I'd painted. Hunting for the hidden gaslighting devices.

I find them, of course.

The Boolean Operators' disembodied voices tell me where to look.

Lead pipes entombed in the ceiling over my bed, set up to thump away in the night.

Hologram-beaming light crystals embedded in the caulking around the false-panel door I'd installed in my bedroom. It leads to a panic room, just big enough for Mickey and me.

Photostatic towels soaked with mind-altering chemicals linked to a heating element when I tear apart my stereo components.

NINE-AND-A-HALF: THEORIES

When it comes to a serious search for evidence of *gaslighting in extremis*, no self-respecting methamphetamine psychotic gashes open a ceiling or takes pliers to a stereo amplifier, only to come up empty. *There is always something there.* I find evidence supporting, never refuting, the theories I construct. The conclusions I'd drawn long before beginning my search for evidence.

A battle is underway.

The Boolean Operators are after me…

I am the hero.

Someone convinced Kim S., sister-in-law of Dave Grohl, to walk past my garage, compliment me. *Someone* compelled her to wear a ring like the one I gave Blossom. To wear a Rolex like the one my mom wears. I don't know who *someone* is. My quest, my duty, is to find out.

The only way to solve the mystery of the Boolean Operators is by going deeper into their world.

My mind is hijacked by psychosis. It refuses to accept the Boolean Operators are the result of psychosis. Instead I believe the Boolean version of Kim S.—Boolean Kim, whose disembodied voice I now hear constantly, along with the rest—is the ringleader of a group of futuristic criminals. Boolean Kim's gang duped my family into paying them to "cure" my methamphetamine addiction. She and her gang "gaslight" me, manipulate my reality, to make me believe I have methamphetamine psychosis. So I will quit meth, and she can take credit.

They talk to me in their disembodied voices. I never stop hearing their voices…

The strange things I saw in the night skies…the meteorites and lightning? Boolean Kim S. and her gaslighters tricked

Boolean Uncle Jupiter into stealing military technology from the Army Psychological Operations cadre of weapons.

The fake newspaper articles? Boolean Kim S. has a DocuTech printer.

The buzzing sounds in my head, the voice calling my name from the front door, my Boolean Dad talking to me through the walls? Boolean Kim S. and her gaslighters following me with their HyperSonic Sound device. Just like I read about in the *New York Times Magazine*.

Boolean Kim S. must be stopped!

She and her team of gaslighters won't simply go away when they get me to quit meth. They will use gaslighting technology and HyperSonic Sound on others.

Maybe even on you.

If I don't stop Boolean Kim, she will not stop until she takes over the world.

Fortunately, there is a simple solution…

If Boolean Kim S. and her gaslighters want me to stop doing meth, then to thwart her—to save the world—I must keep doing meth.

One afternoon I'm lying on the couch, sobbing. Mickey is stretched out by the bay windows, letting the sun warm his fur.

"WHY DO YOU DO SO MANY DRUGS?" the Boolean Operators demand.

I beg them to understand—jabber about how when I'm high on drugs, people stare at me on the bus. They think things about me, and I can't turn off their stares. Being high doesn't make it better. But it makes everything familiar. Drugs give me certainty to outcomes. I am sure—even if only at a *subconscious level*—where the first hit from the meth pipe will lead. The nightmarish world of the meth-fueled Boolean Operators is familiar. Like the Cellar Hole, its fantastic clashes and heroes. In the world of Boolean Operators, the battles are real. I am some twisted form of a hero. The meth addict wasting away his life and his parents' money? Is in reality a crusader against the vastly superior forces of gaslighting.

The Boolean Operators exist in order to explain their existence.

"WE ARE SARDAR DHOOM!" Sardar Dhoom is a death cult. Its disciples torment victims with HyperSonic Sound and gaslighting before kidnapping and torturing them to death in the basement of a wealthy aristocrat's home.

"I HAVE STOLEN THE HOMING DEVICE FROM A BRADLEY FIGHTING VEHICLE!" This is Boolean Uncle Jupiter. "WE WILL HARASS YOU UNTIL YOU STOP DOING METH!"

Boolean Kim S. and her teams of gaslighters tricked a vigilante group into believing I am a rapist.

The Biotech Giant hangs me in effigy on the campus lawn.

The death cults and futuristic motorcycle outlaws set my kidnapping and torture as top priority.

All of it beamed to me in images, like waking dreams. I see the images in my mind. The voices of my tormentors are constant, beamed through HyperSonic Sound. Speakers are hidden behind the drywall. The Boolean Operators' visions are detailed scenes of horrific torture. Medical experiments with vinegar injected into victims' kidneys; death-cults' kidnap victims' skin torn off with pliers; prisoners hung from tree branches into acid vats; mafia chieftains slicing off victims' toes one at a time and sowing their lips together.

Sometimes the victims are people I know.

Sometimes they are my family members.

There are more interactions with police. Hours after sunset, two plainclothes cops pull me over as I turn the Jeep into a meth connect's driveway on 23rd Street near Mission. They shine their spotlight on me and the scene, search my vehicle, ask questions.

"Have you ever been arrested?" One plainclothes wears his hair slicked back, chews a toothpick. His partner shows a bodybuilder physique under a white t-shirt as he rummages through the Jeep.

"I quit my job to remodel my home." I mention the Biotech Giant, as I offer some kind of explanation for the mess of tools and Home Depot bags strewn about the Jeep's interior. Fortunately I'd just searched it myself, looking for a cigarette, and thus knew there were no drugs to be found.

"Maybe you should go back into biotech," the plainclothes says, shaking his head as he lets me go.

One sunny afternoon I call 9-1-1, after jabbering Boolean Operators warn me a woman's cut her arm badly in a nearby apartment…I hear the woman's distress, her partner imploring me to *phone the police*…the cops arrive at my front door, accompanied by a firefighter wielding an axe.

"TELL THEM YOU'RE A METH ADDICT!"

"Look," I begin to tell the lead officer, "I have a problem…"

The police make their way into my home, look around. Luckily I'd just cleaned up that morning, stashed my meth paraphernalia.

"What did you want? Attention?" The lead officer admonishes me, before she and her team leave the scene.

I call 9-1-1 again, one night after I'd cradled my Fender guitar at the Monterey Boulevard picture window and witnessed a seeming intruder, swinging a boom microphone over the backyard fence from the neighbor's yard…she was trying to record me arguing with the Boolean death-cults. I'd given chase, tried to show the cops the escape trail through the woods.

It will be years before I feel the full regret for my actions. Those cops had better things to do…intended victims to protect, communities to serve. Looking back, it may well be I subconsciously wished to put myself near police, because part of me wanted to *be a cop*—or a firefighter, soldier, some sort of protector—to absolve myself of self-blame, for failing to protect the little kid I'd been from the insults and ridicule of the Oakmont bullies. I'd get my chances to work with protectors, serve communities…but as I rip to shreds my home on Monterey Boulevard, looking for surveillance devices, a big part of me is still the kid who agonizingly tried but couldn't find words to say hello to Natalie LaFontaine in the high school hallways.

"I AM YOUR PROMISED ONE," says Boolean Elle. She talks to me through the heating ducts. She is a Boolean version of a woman I worked with at the Biotech Giant. Boolean

Elle's luminescent form floats across the ceiling above my black leather armchair. Our conversations last through the night. My Promised One listens as I tell her of my sadness, the fear of a person who believes his friends and family wanted him incarcerated into a psychiatric ward. Yet can't accept his own role in what transpired.

At Father's Day dinner—two months after the UCSF emergency room—two worlds spin close to one another's orbit. Uncle Jupiter is president of his country club. In the club dining room, buffet tables are laden with more food than the assembled diners could eat in a half-dozen meals. Beyond the floor-to-ceiling windows, the manicured fairways of the golf course the pros play when the PGA tour comes to town. I, wearing a blue wool suit and high on meth, believe the man unwrapping Father's Day gifts, who tried to have me committed to a psychiatric institution, is somehow connected to Boolean Uncle Jupiter, the Mossad spy who planted a grain-of-rice transponder in my neck.

"Uncle Jupiter," I say, after dinner. "What's going on?"

He puts his new pair of tube socks, a gift, into a sack.

"Look…can I at least borrow some money? Forty dollars."

"No, kiddo. No money. Only food. How's the job search going?"

Job search?

Earlier *that same day*, a meth connect asked me to stop at a *specific head shop* on Haight Street and get him a glass pipe. As I parked my motorcycle, a woman walked past…*she is Elle!* The real Elle, my former colleague from the Biotech Giant. I followed her to the supermarket. We spoke for a few minutes.

Idle chitchat—what's going on at the Giant these days. No mention made of any conversations through the heating ducts.

It doesn't occur to me to ask for her email address, to maintain a friendship. Instead I speculate as to why my meth connect sent me to a specific head shop where Elle—the woman I'd been seeing float across my ceilings and hearing talk through the heating ducts—happened to be.

Gaslighting, I decide.

If Elle appeared on Haight Street because the gaslighters sent her, I remain a hero in my fantasy world. Otherwise, I'm just a drug addict who has yet to deal with his problems. I ride to the address my meth connect gave me, drop off the glass pipe. Party for an hour or two. Ride off to the country club for Father's Day dinner.

Who has time to think about a job search?

My bank accounts are drained. I've cashed in my retirement funds. The home on Monterey Boulevard is a burned-out shell. All my possessions destroyed. Everything smashed that could be broken. The German bier stein. The glass bookshelves. Thrown out all my photographs, clothes, paperback books. Anything connected to my old life. I hold a garage sale. The teakwood table, black leather armchair, the Regulator A clock…all of it goes, and for a song.

In the time period of 2003 – 2004, five weddings take place.

Ten of my closest friends.

One couple asks me to be their best man.

I show up to zero of those weddings.

Today I wonder how my friends must've felt as they tried to

explain to their guests, and to themselves, when my name came up during the receptions. The natural human response being to wonder if it was their fault...it wasn't, of course. My friends all encouraged me to be a writer. *I hadn't even attempted to be a writer.* My friends were following their dreams by getting married. How could I show up at their weddings, having failed to even try after my own dream?

I sell the home on Monterey Boulevard. Keep almost all the money my parents loaned me. One of my meth connections arranges for Mickey and me to live in a studio apartment in the Excelsior District. At 700 Paris Street, on the corner of Italy. A tiny box of a place. A basement room with unpainted drywall, linoleum countertops, a shower stall, and one window. That window has a view of the back side of the home on Monterey Boulevard.

I soon discover: The floors are made of Wiggy Wood, a type of gaslighter's tool where the wood grain forms shapes—of monsters, demons, naked women.

For some reason, whoever built the place made these two huge recesses in the wall. Set close together like a massive pair of eyes. So it's like being inside a giant brain. Or, like a monstrous mind is staring at me.

It's in this studio, the Boolean Operators reveal the real, overarching reason they've come for me...

I truly am one of the most important individuals on the planet.

My actions can cause or avert full-scale global war...

I can conceal or reveal a conspiracy at the highest levels of

Nine-and-a-Half: Theories

the most powerful forces on Earth.

I discover this after I've used some of my parent's money to purchase a laptop. My idea is to write a book; instead I download torture porn. But I also navigate to the FBI website. Believing the Boolean Operators were sent by criminals and the FBI can help me.

"YOU MAY WANT TO CHECK OUT THE PICTURES OF THE SEPTEMBER ELEVENTH HIJACKERS," the Boolean Operators say.

And as I do, my heart skips beats, my stomach drops, and it feels like the Earth is tilted the wrong way on its axis.

Staring back at me from the FBI website, is a familiar face. The name is different—*Satam al Suqami*—but to me, the picture looks just like Omar. My friend from Bangkok.

"YOU WERE THE BEST FRIEND OF ONE OF THE HIJACKERS! OR SO DOES IT SEEM…"

It's clear why the Boolean Operators came for me, the reasons behind the gaslighting.

The Boolean Operators were sent by the FBI.

Ten:
The FBI

Fidelity, Bravery, and Integrity

—Motto of the FBI

The Boolean Operators use the voices of FBI agents to tell me Omar was an undercover operative—working for the French, or the Mossad.

Bangkok, Thailand, 2000... "Omar" to my right

"HE INFILTRATED THE TERRORIST CELLS!"

There's a coverup; I know too much; am targeted for neutralization....

Ten: The FBI

"YOUR FRIEND OMAR WAS TRULY A TERRORIST!"

I have been secretly recruited to work for the FBI.

The FBI—according to the Booleans—conducts a vast "war game" to train agents in domestic counterterrorism. My Boolean FBI handlers instruct me via subliminal messaging and hypnotic cues.

"THE FBI CONSIDERS YOU A TOP ASSET!"

The Booleans are my companions, advisors, friends, enemies, sparring partners. The city of San Francisco is the playing field. My role is Lone Wolf terrorist. I'm not supposed to *be* a terrorist, of course. I'm supposed to stalk around *looking like* one. Thus, the disembodied voices of Americans pouring through my studio walls. Friends and families of 9/11 victims, voices filled with hatred, accusing me of terrible crimes.

"YOU WERE SATAM AL SUQAMI'S BEST FRIEND!"

"YOU CAUSED SEPTEMBER ELEVENTH! YOU HELPED PLAN THE ATTACK!"

I scream at my empty studio, at the eye-cutouts. Rage like spewing lava as I stoke my meth pipe and Mickey flees to the shower stall. I've stopped abusing Mickey, although I still neglect him at times. He hides in the shower, knowing I'll soon be flipping over furniture, breaking any glass left unbroken. The mirrors on the closet sliding doors, the oven window—I've hurled 12-volt batteries torn from shredded electronics. I've shattered it all.

"The FBI should come to me in person!" I scream. Then start sobbing. "They should *tell me* I'm part of their war game."

The Booleans become sympathetic. "IF YOU KNEW IT WAS A WAR GAME, YOU WOULDN'T BE SUCH A GOOD ACTOR."

"But I'm not acting!"

"EXACTLY!"

The voices morph into a bass menace, rise to a strychnine whine. They stream from the recessed light fixtures, hum from the refrigerator Freon's special chemistry, brewed in an FBI lab to carry the Boolean's amplitudes.

"YOU ARE A SPY!" the voices scream. "RESPONSIBLE FOR NINE-ELEVEN! WE ARE HERE TO BRING YOU TO JUSTICE!"

"I'm not a spy!" I scream back, spitting curses.

"THEN YOUR PARENTS ARE A SPY!"

"You mean my parents are *spies*."

"SO, YOU FREELY ADMIT OF IT?"

"No!" I yell. "I mean, grammatically…"

The Boolean Operators exist in order to explain their existence.

The FBI had contacted my family to enlist their help in training me, eliminating me, silencing me. My family, having learned Omar was a Mossad agent, sold the information to the terrorists. The Booleans are here to make me the fall guy.

The FBI uses me as bait, allows the most powerful criminal organizations to come after me—I am the only one who can help stop them. And they must be stopped. With their HyperSonic Sound, futuristic technology, and networks of followers, they have the potential to rain destruction upon innocent people everywhere. The Booleans are here to keep me company, to serve as my guides.

"BECAUSE YOU HAD CONTACT WITH SATAM AL SUQAMI, A KNOWN TERRORIST," they say, voices full of joy, "THE FBI CAN LEGALY CONDUCT SURVEILLANCE

Ten: The FBI

UPON YOUR PERSON!"

"But…Suqami was Omar, a counterterrorism agent…"

"YOU ARE ONE OF THE FEW GUARDIANS OF THE SECRET."

I nod and pull smoke from my meth-pipe.

"YOU ARE A HERO TO INTENDED VICTIMS EVERYWHERE."

The Boolean FBI catches the outlaws and, Hydra-like, more take their place.

The news media is in on my gaslighting campaign. The Benjamin Vanderford hoax video comes out. (Vanderford faked his own beheading at the hands of terrorists in Iraq; I believe pictures of him on the internet are doctored pictures of me.)

I smoke more meth; the Boolean Operators keep coming.

I am terrified, miserable, filled with hate…

And completely at home in my Boolean surroundings.

Comfort does not equal happiness.

I play a role I never thought possible. At the nexus of some fantastic world, far beyond anything I could've dreamed up in the Cellar Hole. Certain I'm deeply involved with the FBI. Either wrongfully perused and thus a champion of justice…

Or, an indispensable player in an effort to bring to justice some of the most terrifying criminals in history.

Whatever scenario I happen to believe at any given time, I am a grandiose presence.

My mother sends me a newspaper clipping about a big fire in downtown Ashburnham. I spend hours scanning the photograph for subliminal images. My father sends me letters on philosophy. I search the text for codes and double meanings.

Lynn calls me to ask about the hallucinations she'd heard I was having. I believe she's trying to *induce hallucinations.*

I call my mom. We talk about an article in the *New Yorker.* As if it was another idle Sunday afternoon before a new week at the Biotech Giant. I don't tell her I used some of her money to buy a sawed-off shotgun from a meth connect on the run from the Hells Angels. Carried the firearm home under my long coat, stopping at Safeway for a pint of ice cream along the way.

Mornings I come to with the shotgun resting on my chest. It was how I'd passed out, waiting for FBI-hired gangsters to kick down my door, come to kidnap and torture me to death.

"WE MUST ELIMINATE YOU. YOU KNOW TOO MUCH!

"WE ARE SORRY," the Booleans add.

I'm stalked by vigilante citizens' groups. They've been led to believe by the Boolean FBI that I helped the terrorists. Enraged I'm walking the streets a free man, the vigilantes use HyperSonic Sound to scream at, insult, and threaten me.

A friend emails me a picture from the website www.omsex.com. It's of a man attacking a woman sitting at a spinning wheel, about to rape her. The man is a doctored picture of me, taken on the street when I shook Mickey by the scruff of the neck. Mickey has been airbrushed out. Yet behind the rapist are pictures of dogs on a fireplace mantle. The room in which the rape is to take place is my parents' living room.

Thus, my friends and family are with the FBI on the gaslighting.

"WE ARE HERE TO MAKE YOU QUIT SMOKING METH, YOU TINY BOY!" My Boolean Uncle Jupiter rages

Ten: The FBI

at me. "WE WILL KILL MICKEY!"

"THE FBI IS AFTER YOU," shouts my Boolean cousin Lynn. "YOU HELPED THE TERRORISTS! DON'T YOU THINK YOU SHOULD QUIT SMOKING METH?"

I buy three cars in rapid succession. Two are towed away, one stolen. The stereo equipment and guitars, I either smash in fits of rage or sell for a fraction of their value when the money and meth run out.

I take a taxi to a North Beach strip club, knowing I can't pay the fare. Leave my Apple laptop and Coach leather satchel with the driver (I'd brought the laptop to show my strip club "girlfriend" evidence of the FBI gaslighting). Agreeing to call him the next day, pay the fare, get my belongings back. But the next day, the number is disconnected. I am terrified the cab driver is a foreign agent, and the FBI will send me to prison for espionage, planting fake evidence on my computer.

Boolean Dave Grohl talks to me through the walls. He got taken in by the Boolean FBI when they tried gaslighting his best friend. "THEY PROMISED IT WOULD HELP," Boolean Dave says. "WE TRIED TO SAVE KURT." A Boolean FBI agent reruns the audio recordings, allowing me to listen in on the lonely last conversations between Kurt and his own Boolean Operators.

Boolean Dave Grohl gives me guitar lessons, promises me we'll jam in person someday. Boolean Dave is a funny guy. Sometimes filled with unbridled enthusiasm, encouraging my efforts at musicianship. Then he'll fly into a rage or descend into sullenness at my inability to figure out why the Boolean Operators came for me.

Boolean Elle, my Promised One, claims she is being held hostage, or has been duped into appearing on a TV reality show, or tricked into marrying my Boolean arch-rival. I must save her, claim her love for my own.

"YOU ARE PROMISED TO BOOLEAN ELLE! WE ARE HERE TO ENSURE A UNION!"

With Mickey leashed at my side, I race through San Francisco's streets, following the sweet sound of my Promised One's voice. Desperate to find a way to express love. Or Boolean Elle and I will talk through the walls. As the Boolean FBI zeros in on the nightmarish criminals with HyperSonic Sound beamed at my Excelsior window. At one point, Elle's disembodied voice tells me she's being held hostage at the Bank of America on Van Ness and Market. By super-criminals, bent on stealing my "inheritance." With my .357 tucked in my waistband, I *arrive at the bank* to try and save her.

"Where is the inheritance meeting being held?" I implore the bewildered branch manager. "Is there an upstairs conference room?" He slowly shakes his head. I—fortunately—find the sense to go home.

Home in my box of a studio, smoking meth all night, I scream at the Boolean Operators, countering their threats and accusations. Fending off their global conspiracies. It's a world like the one I should've created in the pages of a book. A world in which *I am important.* My studio walls seem to constrict like a snake's belly as the giant eye socket cutouts' dead gaze hovers above. A skull in a ritual grave.

Ten: The FBI

All my money is gone. I have nothing left to feed Mickey. I come to on the couch, late afternoon. During a cold weather snap, I'd found a family of dead mice under the cushions. They must've crawled in for warmth and frozen there.

My front-tooth stayplate bothers me. For years I've been using the dental apparatus, like dentures except only the one front tooth. It's rubbing the roof of my mouth raw, so I rip it out and hurl it across the floor. Now missing a front tooth, I tuck my .357 into my waistband—I've been carrying it everywhere, as protection, terrified of gangsters or cult members kidnapping and torturing me to death. It's a massive pistol. Holds eight rounds in the cylinder, cold gray steel and black grip. I leash Mickey. We walk the few blocks to Rich's apartment, my meth connect.

He lets me in, reluctantly. Reluctant acceptance is the best I can hope for wherever I go. After we've smoked a few bowls, I take my father's Rolex off my wrist and hand it to him.

"What's it worth?"

He turns it over in his hands. "The crystal is cracked," he says. "It has to be replaced."

"But it's a Rolex," I plead. "It still has value."

"The clasp, here? It's bent."

"You can just bend it back, and it's fine...it was worth something once....c'mon, Rich," I beg.

At my court hearing two months later, I won't care I traded my father's Rolex for a sixteenth of meth. When the prosecutor informs the judge the cops found 1.1 grams on me, I'll be upset Rich shorted me! A sixteenth is supposed to be 1.75 grams.

I leave Rich's apartment and head to the supermarket. Mickey trots alongside. We arrive at Cala Foods. I take the leather loop from my wrist and secure it to the steel corral where the shopping carts stack. As Mickey gazes after me, hoping to get fed soon, I go into the store and steal a package of hamburger.

The security guard follows me into the parking lot.

He's an older man, smaller than I. He grabs at my jacket. I pull away and unleash Mickey.

"I don't want to beat you!" the guard shouts. "Stop walking!"

I ignore him. He draws his Maglite from his belt. It looks as big as an iron girder when he swings it at my head. I raise my arm…I learned the block freshman year in college, in a one-unit taekwondo class. That October night in the Cala Foods parking lot, the block is the first thing from college I've used in years. When I raise my arm, my jacket rides up; the guard must see my .357…soon after, the police arrive. In force.

The squad car whips onto Brazil Street from Mission, cutting off my path. Officer Pagano leaps out, gun pointed at my head. I'm not worried, knowing she won't shoot me so long as I comply with her instructions.

Pagano: "Tie the dog up!" I set the hamburger on a Volkswagen bumper and wrap Mickey's leash around a parking meter.

"Do you have anything sharp in your pockets?" Cops ask before searching you, to avoid injuries (theirs or yours) from any knife blade, syringe, etc., you may be carrying.

"No," I reply. "But there's a loaded pistol in my waistband."

As Officer Pagano's taking the gun from me, Mickey *eats the hamburger*. Destroys the evidence.

"MAN'S BEST FRIEND!"

Ten: The FBI

Mickey will end up serving sixty days in the kennel on an obstruction of justice beef. It's a story to laugh about at the retelling. But as Officer Pagano loads me into her squad car and drives me away, I force myself not to look at Mickey, tied to the parking meeting on Mission and Brazil Streets. He has less an idea than I do what might be happening.

An hour later, I'm shackled to a steel rail in the Ingleside Police Station. The room is bare and covered in smooth tile. Officer Pagano sits to my right. She pushes a button on a tape recorder, begins her interview. "I appreciate your honesty. About the gun. Did you steal the hamburger?"

"No," I lie. "I had it with me."

"What about the gun?"

"I needed it for protection."

"From who?"

Tears stream down my cheeks, I can't stop them, don't want to stop them. I once read an ex-junkie author explain how when you fall, it's always when you run out of money, not before. I've fallen, all right.

"Why are you crying?" Officer Pagano wants to know. There's a weird feeling she thinks it's because I shot someone. I'm not concerned. I didn't shoot anyone; nobody will believe I did.

"I'm worried about my dog." It's the truth, no matter how idiotic it might sound.

"We'll take care of your dog," she says. "Animal Care and Control probably picked him up already." She turns off the tape recorder, knowing she'll get nothing of value from me. "Look," she says, "I hope you get back on track." She leaves the room.

I hope you get back on track.

It's almost a throwaway line…

But the way Officer Pagano says it makes me realize something.

She cares about me.

Insofar as she cares about human beings in general, and I—even if just barely—fit into that category. Ironic; the person whose concern for the human race gives a burned-out criminal meth addict (me) the small yet powerful reminder of his own humanity, wears a police uniform.

It's a small yet meaningful lesson…

From different walks of life, we can come together to improve ourselves.

Soon, another human being, from a far different walk of life from Officer Pagano's, will reinforce the lesson.

Eleven:
Imprisonment & Freedom

Boolean Operators are used to connect and define the relationship between your search terms.

—Website of the Albany University Library

"It's my favorite scene from any movie," the voice says. "She left her husband…but it was to save him."

It's dark in the Big House kitchen workers' dorm. My eyes are closed. But I know the voice. It belongs to a bearded, African-American inmate. *A fellow inmate.* With a physique such that you might look up from an NFL line of scrimmage to see him playing a solid middle linebacker. Late at night, San Bruno County Jail. I'd been sleeping, until *the talk of two fellow inmates* woke me.

I open my eyes.

My fellow inmates sit at the submarine-hull tables. Silhouettes in the gloom, a few feet away. Our shared home, the Big House, a football field of crumbling concrete and peeling pipes. Surrounding rusty metal bunk beds, ghosts of interred Japanese, wreckage of future lives of prisoners. The vast majority African American.

"See," the voice says, "she wanted her husband to live his

dream. The movie never comes right out and tells you. But it was what she wanted."

"I used to have an inflatable woman." This voice is unfamiliar. "She was the best. We never had no arguments, no issues…"

"Man, that's not what I'm talking about. In the movie, see, she had underlying motivations."

"My inflatable girl, she had underlying motivations too, if you know what I mean. My homie, he wanted an inflatable woman. But when I told him she cost seventy-five dollars, he said, 'I ain't paying seventy-five dollars for no booty!'"

The irony might be worth reflecting upon, in another time and place. But in the middle of the night in San Bruno County Jail, my sense of entitlement kicks in. *Who do these guys think they are, talking when I wanna sleep?* Rage boils. I fail to consider: If I hadn't allowed myself to become a meth addict, hadn't carried a pistol and stolen hamburger from Cala Foods, I wouldn't find my sleep disturbed here in jail.

My standard response when the entitlement feelings kick in is to send crude non-verbal signals. Scowls, grunts. Hoping not only to convey the way I feel but that others will understand and act accordingly. Always the other person who needs to change. Yet in jail, a scowl or grunt means even less than on the outside. I leap from my bunk, yank open the metal drawer that serves as my storage space, slam it hard. The sound like a gunshot in the dim light of the Big House.

"You got a problem?" the bearded inmate wants to know.

You could say I do.

I'm primed to fight. Unusual…most times when I carry on, physical violence is unlikely. My audience is non-combatants

Eleven: Imprisonment & Freedom

(friends, family, etc.). But in the Big House, it's one of the few times when despite all my bluster, my bullying others the way those Oakmont kids bullied me, it might actually come to blows.

Not caring about the consequences, I take a step forward, ball my hand into a fist...

Boom!

The dormitory lights come on...

It's 2:00 a.m. Time for our kitchen shift to start.

There'll be no violence. Fortunate for the bearded inmate. Had we fought, he might've suffered severely bruised knuckles against my skull and ribs.

I work my kitchen shift. Later, a veteran inmate takes me aside. Gerry's a solid biker, martial artist, wears a Fu Manchu mustache and slicked-back hair. Bounced in and out of jail for many years. The terms of his probation prevent him from being in possession of so much as a metal paint scraper. Gerry and I play gin rummy; he talks mostly about his wife, his home life. But today, after kitchen shift, the look in his biker eyes is of concern.

"That guy you almost tussled with, with the beard? His name is Two Jacks."

"Two Jacks?" I dab at my forehead with my jail-issue towel, at beads of sweat from the kitchen steam.

"Yeah," Gerry says. "He's pretty upset. You better apologize. I might not be around next time..." Gerry shrugs. I catch his drift. Two Jacks has something in store for me. We're not talking an extra serving of powdered eggs on the chow line, either.

Two Jacks lies on his bunk. At the far end of the block and near the bathrooms. The furthest point from the sheriff's deputies' station. The bathrooms are where the fights go down. Two Jacks is cocooned in a blanket. Only the top of his head and his eyes poke out. *But are those eyes open?* I'm staring... and yes, his eyes are indeed open. Looking right at me. But by now I've been staring...*as if in challenge*...far too long. And somehow it doesn't seem right to just go up to him while he's blanketed in his bunk.

I keep walking.

Into the bathroom.

The gladiatorial combat area.

By Big House rules, maybe I've just thrown down a gauntlet. Beamed a death-stare at Two Jacks, challenged one of the most veteran inmates to mutual combat. Two of us enter the bathroom; one comes out. Sure, I'd fought in the ring a few times. But there are *rules* in Muay Thai. And I was never much good in the ring anyway. The adrenaline from six hours ago is long gone. I pace a circle or two, flush a urinal, run some water in the sink. No one else here but me.

Back on the block, Two Jacks is standing, arms folded. This may be my last chance to do much of anything in life...

"I wanted to apologize," I tell him. My words are met with a stare. So hard it might be a piece of meteorite made of solid chromium, plunged to Earth after a billion-year trip across the universe. I realize I'm muttering, and it sounds like I'm demanding *he* apologize.

"I mean," I say, "*I apologize*. To you. I'm apologizing." His stare is maybe a softer type of stone. Or very hard wood. "I was having a bad day," I say. "I took it out on you... no hard feelings?"

I extend my hand. He looks at it for a long moment.

Then takes it in a handshake.

Two Jacks becomes my jailhouse mentor. Shows me how to do push-ups with my head near the wall, so no one can kick me in the head. When another inmate steals my boots, I go to Two Jacks. He mediates their return.

One afternoon I'm lying on my bunk, reading *Bonfire of the Vanities*. I'd asked my parents to mail it. I'd read it before, so it's easy to consume in the noise and distractions of jail. Another inmate storms up, enraged. He rips open my locker and begins tearing through it.

"You take my wave cap?" He snarls. A wave cap is like a bandana, worn around the skull.

"I'm white," I say, laughing as I set down my paperback. "We don't wear wave caps." I'm trying to diffuse the tension with a joke. But not sure if the way I've brought race into the equation, is taking the proper tack.

"I don't give a damn if you're white," he says, thrashing through my things.

Two Jacks ambles over. "These are our lockers," he says, calm as the air before a hurricane. The implication is clear.

"I don't give a damn," the other inmate mutters. But he makes a little show of straightening up my stuff, before gently closing my locker door.

"It was good," Two Jacks tells me later, "the way you handled that." I feel a strange sense of pride. For maybe the first time since I ran behind Omar through the tangled Bangkok streets, I've done something well while not on drugs.

In the Big House, we Caucasians are in the extreme minority. African Americans call us "wood." It isn't meant as an insult.

The African Americans call each other "O.G.," Original Gangsta. The Latinos wear white plastic crucifixes and are organized, disciplined. They conduct group exercise sessions, like a precision military unit. There aren't many Asians. One is a good cook; one plays basketball and cards; one stays pretty quiet and keeps to himself, mostly reading books.

Two Jacks leads the Midnight Crew, to which I'm promoted by Deputy Horne. Our supervisor is Senior Deputy Bruce. He brings food from outside. Steaks and lobsters, sometimes. We function as his sous chefs, and we get to eat. It's like the scene in *Goodfellas*, where the gangsters feast in their specially outfitted prison cell.

With the exception of Two Jacks and a couple others, most of us on the coveted Midnight Crew are Caucasian. Does this point to scientific evidence linking race to the ability to boil lobsters? No, it does not. As a Caucasian, I'm given unfair advantages on the outside of the jail walls, where I am part of the majority. And unfair advantages on the inside, where I'm in the minority.

As I get to know Two Jacks, and later, other incarcerated persons, I begin to understand. When I was fourteen and drunk at my aunt's wedding, I made two mistakes. I began succumbing to alcoholism, which led to drug addiction. And, I began to engage in criminal activity. In our society, being an underage drinker, a drug user, defines one as a criminal.

For my mistakes, I am eventually punished with those sixty days in jail. It's a punishment I deserve, to be sure. Yet in our society, others make those same two mistakes. They end up punished with far more time. Years. Decades. Lifetimes.

My pathway was always going to be: college, biotech career,

Eleven: Imprisonment & Freedom

home ownership. I had to work hard to get off that path, into addiction and brief incarceration. In our society, others have to work just as hard as I did—much harder, in many cases—to get off the paths society puts them on, into places like higher education and business ownership.

Society gave me unfair advantages. Because of…let's face it…the color of my skin. And my socio-economic background. Now, these things sound obvious, but it's different when you live them. And I got a chance to live them.

The lessons from jail won't crystallize for years to come.

But there will be other, immediate changes.

On that November day in 2004, after showing Uncle Jupiter my slide presentation in the Visitors' Room as Deputy Horne sat nearby with his arms folded across his crisp uniform…I sit at the steel table in San Bruno County Jail. With my legal pad in front of me and my head free from drugs for about a month, I decide to take some kind of a stand.

I begin to write.

What could I possibly have that you might want to read about?

I write a letter to the FBI *(*Note: My letter was actually to the Secret Service, eventually it got passed along to the FBI).

I describe Omar. How I knew him, how he looked like the photograph of Satam al Suqami. The letter states facts—leaving out guesses, accusations, theories. It's one of many pieces of correspondence I will send to the U.S. Intelligence Community. Using language along the lines of, Omar "may have been affiliated" with the terrorists…despite the Boolean Operators' constant insistence Omar *was, without a doubt,* other than whom he claimed. My letter may not be much, but it's a way of *trying to do the right thing*. If I can learn to exist among my fellow humans in jail...to use the opportunity as a starting point to transform my selfishness, mistakes, and take-my-blessings-for-granted attitude...maybe I can apply the same thinking to the story of Omar.

To be clear, it's highly unlikely I would've thought Omar had anything to do with the terrorists, had it not been for the Boolean Operators, the gaslighting.

I'd contacted the Bureau before, about the gaslighting conspiracies. Sent emails, letters, showed up at the FBI offices with "evidence." I never sent anything threatening, or anonymously. But until that jailhouse letter, I mostly cared about what the authorities might do for me. Rarely what I could for them.

"WE ARE HAPPY TO WITNESS YOUR SHIFT IN THINKING!"

Without the meth, the Boolean Operators retreat to a semi-constant presence. They no longer threaten me. They do not sound like people I know or like celebrities. The Boolean Operators are like a chorus of somewhat androgynous voices that encourage my attempts at positive change.

Ironic, I think of my time in jail as being my first steps to freedom...

Because my time in jail marks the start of my recovery.

I'm drug-free for the longest stretch in a decade-and-a-half...

And semi-started on a path to achieving my dream.

I don't intend to make my jailhouse letter to the FBI the start of my writing career. But I'll go on to become a writer...or at least make my best attempt at it. There will be some success, but first there will be failures.

Twelve:
Haikus

...everything in life is writable about if you have the outgoing guts to do it, and the imagination to improvise. The worst enemy to creativity is self-doubt.

—Sylvia Plath

My court date arrives. Five days before Christmas. Uncle Jupiter rises from his seat in the courtroom gallery to speak on my behalf. "We want my nephew to get his life back together. To get back to work." He mentions the Biotech Giant. I know what he wants for me. Promotions. Money in the bank.

Who can blame him? I played along for years.

"YOU'LL BECOME A WRITER!" the Booleans reassure me. "OR AN UNDERCOVER FBI OPERATIVE!"

The judge smashes his gavel. "Mr. Kressy," he says, "it says here," he waves a small stack of papers, "you have an intake appointment at the Henry Ohlhoff House? That's drug rehab, correct?"

"Yes. Yes, Your Honor."

"I don't want to see you back here in an orange jumpsuit, Mr. Kressy."

You're not the only one.

The judge sentences me to time served and three years' probation. There's a few hours' wait in a holding cell as the sheriff's department processes my release. Anger, sense of entitlement kicking in...*why is it taking so long? The judge said I am free to go.* I fantasize about screaming at the sheriff's deputies, demanding my rights. As usual, in no way considering: If I'd never done meth, I would never have ended up behind bars in the first place.

"ITS TYPICAL," the Booleans say, "FOR AN UNDERCOVER OPERATIVE TO SPEND EXTRA TIME IN JAIL."

"PART OF THE TRAINING," the Booleans say. "IT BUILDS CREDIBILITY! ONE MUST HAVE A COVER IDENTITY THAT MIRRORS AS CLOSELY AS POSSIBLE ONE'S ACTUAL LIFE."

Psychosis—mine, anyway—gives you all these special little insights into how the top-secret universe functions. My jail paperwork gets finished, my belongings returned. The clothes I was arrested in feel like old friends. A few Marlboros remain in a pocket of my Ben Davis shirt. I keep the orange jail t-shirt and orange socks, maybe as souvenirs. The sheriff's department releases me to the streets just before nightfall.

My parents are waiting for me at Uncle Jupiter's place. But I take my time. Stop for a slice of Blondie's Pizza, smoke my cigarettes, hang around Market and Powell Streets. Tourists congregate, standing in line for cable cars to ferry them atop a San Francisco hill, back down the other side. Holiday shoppers flood the streets. Carrying bags of gifts and cups of steaming coffee drinks. I picture little kids ripping open presents, smiles of delight. I finish my Marlboro and check my pack: Empty.

The Boolean Operators: "WE'RE SO HAPPY! YOU ARE OUT OF JAIL. WE WOULD'VE STAYED IN THERE WITH YOU LONGER, YOU KNOW."

Yes. Indeed you would've. It's a stern reminder of the possibility of an FBI frame-up. *Prison for life.* A vast cover-up of the true identity of Satam al Suqami. I scan for the agents certain to be following me. Back at San Bruno, informants had posed as jail inmates. Perpendicular Planes had appeared during yard time softball. Several people at the cable car turnaround look like FBI types. No way to tell for sure. No use trying to do anything about it. Any loss of control might mean another trip to the UCSF emergency room, another attempt to have me committed.

A panhandler wearing a dirty orange-and-blue Denver Broncos shirt squats near the doorway of a Chinese restaurant. A clean-shaven tourist in a flawless tan overcoat drops a dollar and change into his outstretched hand. I descend the stairs to the MUNI station. The K line train glides through the underground tunnel to the West Portal Station. Near Forrest Hills, where some of the wealthiest San Franciscans live. I recheck my Marlboro pack. Still empty. I often hide my meth between the cardboard and foil. Had I done that with my sixteenth before getting arrested, maybe the police wouldn't have found it.

I ring Uncle's Jupiter's doorbell. Used to be, I could access a hidden spare key. Those days are gone. Sixty days' jail time for firearms and meth possession cured my family of any ideas I should have free access to their homes.

Uncle Jupiter and Aunt Koral's living room is filled with furniture and artwork accumulated from various around-the-world stops in his Army career. Carved wood, painted canvas, and glassware make a house a home. Pink carpet and white walls. The windows offer views of comfortable dwellings in valleys on hillsides. If it weren't dark, you could see the Pacific. Maybe the spot on Ocean Beach where Mark Burnsen and I drove to…where America ends.

Vague memories of an evening spent with family on the evening of release from jail…

…entering Uncle's Jupiter's living room and announcing, "I haven't sat on a couch in months," like it's the most critical observation possible. Well, it's true, isn't it? I'd come to on my couch with the eye socket drywall cutouts, flung my stayplate across the Excelsior studio. Sitting on my uncle's couch, I use my tongue to probe the gap where my front tooth was. In jail, it hadn't mattered; a lot of guys missing teeth. You'd lie on your rusted-metal bunk and foam-rubber mattress with the stuffing showing through. Your fellow inmate would pad in jail-issue canvas shoes across the grimy cement to ask you about getting up a game of gin rummy at the steel tables, showing you his deck of fifty-one cards…

…cousin Lynn appearing with a handful of take-out menus: "We're ordering dinner." The usual confusion as menus are scanned, too many restaurants, various items chosen.

…Aunt Koral buzzing between the kitchen and living room, fixing drinks, making small talk. Who showed up at her tennis game that morning, plans for the annual spa retreat with her two sisters.

Twelve: Haikus

...seeing my mom for the first time in *what, eighteen months?* Remembering the late-night call I'd made, high on meth, screaming curses into her answering machine. I'd made a passing attempt to apologize from a jail pay phone. "I had nothing to do with September eleventh, mom!"

She'd interrupted me: "I know it was the drugs talking."

...taking my dad off to the side, asking him: "When you lost your job, what was it for?" It's a long-ago memory. I was seven or so. My dad came home one day and announced he'd been fired by his community college. Me, so young and thinking he'd actually been *on fire*. I'd pictured him in his office, engulfed in flames.

"I was trying to form a teachers' union," my dad tells me, there in Uncle Jupiter's living room.

"So, the administration was union-busting." I'm trying to be conspiratorial, to engage us into us-versus-them, manly, hearty talk. I've always tried to connect with my dad, show off knowledge of mechanical matters and intellectual affairs, worldliness and savvy. The way fathers and sons connect on television shows.

"It was a difficult time," my father says. "You and Blossom were very young, and we didn't have a lot of money." He believes my question was an invitation to open up. He can't be expected to know the reason I asked is: I believe after he lost his job, the FBI put him on the payroll in the interests of protecting national security by supporting the unions. *Someone in my family will reveal the FBI conspiracy* I'm certain they're all involved in. *If I just ask the right questions.*

"IF YOU JUST ASK THE RIGHT QUESTIONS!"

The Cellar Hole might've been a few leaping steps from my parents' round wooden table, but the Boolean Operators sit right with me at Uncle Jupiter's. I face the glass display case filled with knickknacks collected from decades of global travel. There's a silver Tiffany clock my mom and her sister Anne got Jupiter for his birthday. It has their names inscribed.

"Uncle Jupiter," I say, "my birthday is coming up. Are we having a dinner?" It's a family tradition at Jupiter's. Going back to when I'd turned eighteen, my first year in college, and they'd served me my "first beer." Every subsequent year I'd invite a bunch of friends and make a big show of refusing beer, trying to pass myself off as a non-drinker. One year, I was high on mushrooms. Now I'm fresh out of my first jail stretch at thirty-four.

"How's your resume coming along?" Uncle Jupiter thinks my problems can be solved with a job. I think they can be solved with a birthday dinner. So, there's something we have in common: We're both wrong.

Later, Lynn and I are outside the house. I stare at the sky. A Perpendicular Plane appears. "Look!" I say, pointing, spouting some gibberish, hoping I'll hit on the right catchphrase or code words to trigger her into admitting, yes, the FBI is up there, following me.

Late at night in the guest bedroom, sandwiched between a mattress and goose-down comforter…for the first time in sixty days, not sharing the Big House dorm with fifty other inmates. I've spent many nights in the bedroom. A few months when I worked as a bike messenger. Smoking grass on the porch before pedaling downtown to deliver packages to law firms. Planning the book I'd write, that never got started.

I toss and turn in the bed, thinking about what kind of book I might write now. About jail, about drugs. About the FBI conspiracies. *A book about the Boolean Operators.*

"ARE YOU GLAD TO BE OUT OF JAIL?"

"Yes," I whisper. "I sure am. Listen…I'm an undercover FBI operative, right?"

"INDEED! A TRUE OPERATIVE RESTS BETWEEN THE COVERS."

Consoled, I fall asleep. I'll write my book someday. Someday the FBI conspiracy will be revealed to me. The Booleans have promised as much.

Mickey is free to go, having served his sixty days in the kennel. We spring him loose, walk around the parking lot, sit in the shade. Mickey's tongue lolls out, a big chunk of dirt hanging from it. I brush it away; he rolls onto his back for a belly rub. His fur is like the snow-capped peak of Mount Fuji below the fuselage window. Later that afternoon, my father, Mickey, and I hike up Mount Davidson. San Francisco stretches out before us—there's the ocean, the USF church, the Pyramid. My father goes off to do his tai chi routine. Two guys nearby are engaged in a telltale semi-surreptitious routine. Half-hiding the pot pipe they pass back and forth.

What the hell, I think. *How much can couple hits hurt?*

Although I don't really *want to be* high…

"C'mon, Mickey." I give a little tug on the leash. We approach with lack of caution. "I just got out of the joint," I tell the pot-smokers. Holding up my arm, showing them the jail ID wristband I haven't bothered to remove. "Can I get a hit?"

I don't know if my father sees me smoking while he's doing tai chi, or if he gets any sense I'm high when we hike back down the mountain. It doesn't matter. I've proven to myself I'm capable of successful interactions with other humans. I may not be able to navigate a family dinner at Uncle Jupiter's, but I can show a jail ID wristband and convince strangers to get me high.

The next day, my parents and Uncle Jupiter bring me to the Ohlhoff House. We park near a laundromat. A young woman exits, carrying a basket of clothes.

"Hey," I say, coming alongside her, matching her stride. "That looks heavy. Can I carry it for you?"

"Sure," she says, smiling. "I live right over there." She hands me the basket. A pair of socks almost falls out.

"I used to live around here." I talk with my lips close together, hiding my missing front tooth. "When I went to college."

"I'm gonna go back to college," she says. "Someday."

"You know those Victorians, on the postcards?"

"Sure. Everyone does."

"That's where I'm headed." I shift the clothes basket, adjusting my grip.

"Wow!" She laughs. "You must have an expensive life."

We reach her apartment. I leave the clean laundry on the steps leading up to the front door.

The Ohlhoff House is a monster Victorian—breathtaking, dozens of windows, conical roof peaks. One imagines it built after Gold Rush days, as testimony to a clan's traveling thousands of miles across a hostile continent…journeying toward a land known only through dreams and promises; surviving soul-crushing hardships to prosper in the land of riches. Of course we've often forgotten the fortunes of those native to the fields and forests. I climb the stone steps; my parents and Uncle Jupiter follow me.

A guy sits, smoking. "Hey," I say. "This is the Ohlhoff House, right?" Even though I already know the answer.

"Welcome to paradise, buddy." I get the feeling he made the same trip up the stone steps. His family in tow and a lifetime of wreckage behind him. We shake hands, wish each other Happy Holidays. Inside, the receptionist gives me a few forms and a pen. My parents and uncle take seats in the lobby as the receptionist points me towards the TV room. The furniture is old, and the Oriental rug is threadbare. A guy wearing jeans and a flannel shirt stares at the TV, looking like a zombie. *Probably the way I look,* I realize.

"THIS IS A PLACE WE COULD CALL HOME!" the Boolean Operators say. "WE LOVE IT HERE!"

My parents fly back to Massachusetts on Christmas Day. I guess they figure it will be an easier trip, the flights less crowded. It doesn't matter. There's Mickey, the Boolean Operators—we'll have a great holiday together! I've decided not to check in to the Ohlhoff House. Who would take care of Mickey if I did? I should've been asking, who would take care of me if I *didn't.*

Boolean Dave Grohl gives me a few drum lessons, teaches me to tap out rhythms with open palms and footfalls on the floor. The Boolean FBI sends Perpendicular Planes in lieu of Santa's sleigh.

I write another letter to the authorities, further information about Omar. This one composed on Lynn's computer. *There must be a way to build a bridge between the Boolean world and the other one.*

The mind finds what it seeks…

If you remember, one of the hijacker's passports was found on the sidewalk at Ground Zero. This passport belonged to Satam al Suqami.

A man named Daniel Lewin was a passenger on American Airlines Flight 11. Lewin served four years as a captain in a special forces units of the Israeli Defense Forces. Reportedly, Lewin was stabbed to death by one of the hijackers. The hijacker who reportedly stabbed him, was Satam al Suqami.

The *9/11 Commission Report* describes Suqami as "…unconcerned with religion, and…known to drink alcohol."

"LIKE OMAR! HE SAID HE DRANK BEER."

The *9/11 Report* tells us Suqami flew into Iran from Bahrain in November 2000. Which, technically, would've allowed Omar to get to Bangkok in late November of that year, when I met him.

Most people who've seen Omar's photograph say he doesn't look much like Suqami. Yet the *9/11 Report* states "…the passports of Satam al Suqami and (hijacker) Abdul Aziz al Omari were recovered after 9/11. Both had been doctored."

Of course, the *Report* does not specify the passport *photographs* had been doctored…

The mind finds what it seeks.

Twelve: Haikus

Lynn's work colleague has an apartment for rent at 81 Denslowe Drive. Near San Francisco State University. About a mile from Uncle Jupiter's. My parents pay my rent and the deposit. Lynn helps me move what few things I've kept from the Excelsior studio. As we're unloading her car, she catches me sneaking a cigarette break. Standing in the crushed gravel, resting my foot on the stone tortoise that silently guards the driveway.

"Hey!" Her voice edged with anger, disappointment. "What are you doing?"

"Just...smoking." Feeling guilty, I put the cigarette out and bring the rest of my belongings inside.

"So, what are you going to do?" Lynn asks. We're hanging out in the studio. Like we did twenty years before while *The Road Warrior* played on the VCR in her home in Heidelberg.

"Probably just unpack."

"I mean, with your life?"

"It's my life." I don't like the edge in her voice. "I guess I'll do what I want." I open the window and light a cigarette.

"You can't smoke in here," Lynn says.

"It's my apartment."

"This is my friend's apartment," she says matter-of-factly. I take it to mean because her friend rented it to me, Lynn has more say over what goes on here than I do. Now I'm angry. Lynn keeps pushing. "What are you thinking?" I hear judgment in her voice, I feel like she's demanding I let her fix me. "You don't have a job; you don't have a resume. You don't even have any toilet paper."

It's too much. But I don't know how to express my feelings...

So, I storm out.

"OF YOUR OWN APARTMENT!"

"Come on, Mickey." I grab him by the collar, stomp around looking for his leash. "Let's go get Lynn her toilet paper...let's make sure she's happy." My voice is barely below a shout.

My cousin Lynne is *right* to be upset with me. But I'm thirty-four and operating at the same level of interpersonal communication I've been at all my adult life—that of a somewhat emotionally underdeveloped sixteen-year-old. Sixteen... the age I began drinking heavily. I might as well be a monkey, banging garbage can lids like cymbals. I experience feelings but don't believe they are valid. Don't believe I even *have the right* to feelings. And even if I do, I don't have the faith and confidence in myself to express them. Not in healthy ways, at least. Afraid I'll be seen as weak, stupid, laughable.

When I return to the apartment—forgetting, of course, the toilet paper—Lynn has left. Later she calls and apologizes. "I'm sorry if I pushed your buttons."

"Nice of you to say!" My response sarcastic, wanting her to know that because she's apologizing, I was right all along.

A month passes. Somehow I stay clean off meth. My parents pay for a dentist to forge me a new front-tooth stay plate. I'm in limbo...a drug addict is an island. Disconnected from my family, lost without the familiar comfort of meth. It's okay to hang out with Mickey and the Boolean Operators. Hypnotic drum lessons from Boolean Dave Grohl, routine undercover operative training from the Boolean FBI. The terror that comes from the conspiracy fears, I can manage.

Twelve: Haikus

I accept my psychosis as a normal state of being. What I see in reality only reinforces the fantasy...a Perpendicular Plane glides over San Francisco State as I walk Mickey...an unmarked military aircraft, aqua-blue, incredibly low and quiet.

Even without the meth, it's impossible to shake the paranoia. The FBI is simply stringing me along, waiting to kill me...or worse. My family knows things they aren't telling me. Before I moved to the studio, I stayed at Uncle Jupiter's. I made an appointment with a psychiatrist, at 3874 California Street. But in my notebook, I wrote the address as "387 California," accidentally leaving off the "4" at the end. Eventually I get to the right place. But when I returned to Uncle Jupiter's, someone had gone into my notebook and written in that missing "4."

The psychiatrist gave me a couple forms to fill out, for blood-work and informed consent and such...

But her signature is different on the two forms.

She is with the FBI.

With the gaslighters.

No other explanation.

I believe my family, my doctor, and everyone else keeps secrets from me. They all know about the people I think are after me, about the reasons I hear the Boolean Operators. Allowing myself to think this way is very hard on my psychological processes, will distance me from my family for years to come. But the root of my problems, of course, is *me*. Yes, I feel alienated from my family. Yet I've allowed myself to be in the position where I depend upon them to survive. My parents are paying my rent, therapist visits, groceries, and a-hundred-dollars-a-week spending money.

I need to break free, do something on my own.

Pursue my dream.

San Francisco has a General Assistance program (GA is another term for welfare). My first GA check, I spend on fancy paper, a calligraphy pen, and these special gold paper clips that look like seashells. Kinko's prints up business cards for me. Saturday morning, as the sunshine forces its way through the San Francisco fog, Mickey and I board the bus that lets us off near Galileo High School, just up the hill from Fisherman's Wharf. OJ Simpson went to Galileo. The Wharf is where I had my first job when I came to San Francisco. Where the street performer with the stubble under his face paint smoked his cigarette on the side of the stage.

It's a fitting place to launch my new career as a professional writer.

It's an entrepreneurial idea…

I'll write haikus about random tourists and sell them to those tourists. Like the sketch artists who set up easels facing the ocean. You and your family sit for a charcoal portrait with the Golden Gate Bridge in the background. Except I'm gonna write haikus about tourists *without them knowing*.

"YOU WILL PLY YOUR TRADE FROM AFAR."

Yes. I'll spot some tourists, write a nice haiku about them on the parchment paper, then do my sales pitch: It only takes a few seconds to read a haiku. They'll read the little poem about themselves… they'll be glad to pay me.

"FINDING MODERN-DAY PATRONS OF THE ARTS," the Boolean Operators say. "WE LOVE YOUR IDEA!"

The Boolean Operators come up with a haiku about me:

Twelve: Haikus

"METHAMPHEATAMINE...
HE SMOKED IT ALL THE TIME, THEN
NOW HE WRITES HAIKUS"

Well, *okay*...except haikus are supposed to have a nature reference, right? What do I know, except for what I learned in grade-school English...5-7-5 syllable count, etc.? There on Fisherman's Wharf, I'm probably insulting centuries of artistic tradition. I take a cigarette break before starting work. Rub Mickey's snout as he lies on the sun-warmed sidewalk.

I think about Hunter S. Thompson.

In February 2005, the month I decide to become a professional writer? Thompson puts a shotgun in his mouth and pulls the trigger. His books showed me it's possible for a person to live a life that fascinates the one living it—in the thick of national politics, riding with a Hells Angels club, or the sportswriter's/no-consequences-drug-freewheeler's existence in *Fear & Loathing in Las Vegas*—and transcend his own experiences by giving the reader—me—a glimpse into the possibilities for his own life.

I read somewhere someone blasted Thompson's ashes into space on a rocket. It cost three million dollars. Back in my drug days, I would've paid to see it. Today, I think about the hungry children those dollars might've fed. When I was nineteen and read *Fear & Loathing in Las Vegas*, I was a different sort of hungry. Starving for the idea I could write something like it. Hah! I had a better chance of launching a football league where the players ride unicycles.

Years after quitting meth, I'll get another tattoo beneath the cover art from *Fear & Loathing*. It reads **Adois**. In courier font.

It's "Adiós," Spanish for goodbye, and a riff on the cliché of a misspelled tattoo. On another level...the idea of Thompson, twisted on drugs whilst sitting at his typewriter to write his suicide note...*Adiós*...but the "o" and "i" are too close together on the keyboard, and he's too high. He misspells his one-word farewell. And with that period at the end...final. Indeed. *Adois*, Hunter. In February 2005, I'm on Fisherman's Wharf, trying for both of us.

Mickey and I patrol the sidewalks. A tourist couple strolls outside a shop selling Alcatraz Swim Team t-shirts. To this day it's not certain if Frank Morris and the Anglin brothers made good their 1962 prison break or died trying. I dash off a couple lines of verse on the fancy parchment paper. My handwriting isn't so neat, but that's okay. Haiku in one hand, Mickey's leash in the other, I make my approach.

"What a wonderful dog!" The wife exclaims, petting Mickey. She's got a gray San Francisco sweatshirt and a big sun hat. The husband is stocky, wears a plaid shirt and a friendly, ruddy face.

"Where are you folks from?" I ask.

"Montana," the husband says. "Figured we'd get to California for the winter. Didn't expect it to be so cold. My wife's a teacher. They had to go on strike last fall. Wages too low."

"Beautiful."

He stares at me, smile fixed in place.

"I mean, Montana. It's beautiful."

"So, you've been there?"

"Ah, no...I mean, so I'm told. Look, I have these haikus... they're like Japanese poems."

"Haikus!" The woman looks up from scratching Mickey's

ears. "We've heard of those in Montana."

"I have one about you." I show them the parchment paper. "It's yours...and if you can make a donation..."

My dream since childhood...to be a writer! I don't realize I've already accomplished it, simply by writing. As for my haiku?

The tourists from Montana aren't buying.

Discouragement sets in; no problem. Everyone gets discouraged, right? We pick ourselves up under our own power and move on. But I don't know—indeed, have never known—how to get along when things don't go my way. My family provides what seems like everything—food, shelter, companionship in Mickey, the therapist—these don't give me the feeling I *am somebody*, have something to offer. The dream of being a writer seems impossible after only one failure.

Of course, it wasn't even a failure. I may not have *sold* my writing, but still I had *written*.

It doesn't matter. The version of the FBI my methamphetamine psychosis created...the Boolean Operators turned into the world's worst criminals and me, doing battle against them? With Boolean Dave Grohl at my side, no less. *Satam al Suqami was an infiltrator; he was my friend Omar.*

"YOU ARE A VITAL PLAYER IN A KEY ROLE!"

These worlds are not only real to me but wouldn't even exist if not for me. With Mickey at my side, I sit atop a set of stone steps in Ghiradelli Square and light a cigarette. Calm, confident.

I've made my decision.

I'll use meth again.

Thirteen:

The Interview

Woe to him who, when the day of his dreams finally came, found it so different from all he had longed for!

—Viktor Frankl, *Man's Search for Meaning*

I'm sitting in an FBI interview room. The two agents look tough enough to break all the furniture into little sticks if they want to. Fortunately, they don't want to.

But these guys aren't interested in haikus either.

"NOW YOU ARE GOING TO BE ARRESTED!" Boolean Agent Denton sounds just like the *real* Agent Denton, one of the agents interviewing me. I ignore the voice. The Boolean voice, that is. FBI Agent Denton I pay attention to.

Police mugshot:
After being locked up in the psych ward, for attempted break-in to my uncle's home, to steal valuables for meth money

Thirteen: The Interview

The previous day, my usual Monday morning routine. Wait around my studio at 81 Denslowe Drive until it seems time for Uncle Jupiter to have left for work. Walk Mickey to Jupiter's house. Aunt Koral feeds me, buys me coffee, cigarettes. Brings me to my therapist's office, takes me grocery shopping, and gives me a $100 weekly allowance from my parents. I spend ten dollars on cigarettes, the rest on a sixteenth of meth.

I sat at Koral's dining table with a bowl of Frosted Flakes. Uncle Jupiter's favorite food. The Tiffany clock—the present to my Uncle Jupiter from my mother and aunt—safe in its glass cabinet. Something caught my attention. A scrap of paper. Looking closer, I saw on it written my name, the letters FBI, and "Agent Denton," along with a phone number.

Strange...a phone message here on the dining table. Koral and Jupiter keep pad and paper near the phone for messages. But here was the FBI's message for me on the dining table...

Like someone doesn't want me to see it.

Jupiter and Koral in the employ of the Mossad...Omar worked for the Mossad...the two Craig David hip-hop tunes he played over and over, encoded with subliminal messages that hypnotized me into hearing the Boolean Operators. I was bred since birth into the role of Fall Guy, to serve a lifetime's prison sentence as my family, the spy ring, walked free and mocked me with the grain-of-rice transponder and their Boolean selves.

"Ready to go to your therapist's?" Aunt Koral called from the kitchen.

Startled, folding the scrap of paper into my Carhartt jacket. "Uh...just a minute...can I use the phone?"

"Of course!" Koral sang. "I'll make more coffee."

The Braun coffeemaker starts its gurgle. I take stairs two-at-a-time, to the bedroom I'd slept in after getting released from jail.

What I've been waiting for…the FBI is finally going to tell me why I was given the Boolean Operators.

Agent Denton's voice is smooth, professional. "I called about an e-mail you had sent," he said on the phone. "Can you come in tomorrow talk about it?"

"Yes," I told him, not hesitating.

There was just one problem.

"Here's your allowance," Aunt Koral said as we pulled up outside my therapist's office in Noe Valley. I pocketed the five twenty-dollar bills.

Why did I leave my therapist's office an hour later and score meth, knowing I'd stay up all night before my FBI interview?

Partying on meth was the *known*. My familiar, unhappy existence was comfortable, less frightening than an unknown, potentially happy one. A life outside my comfort zone, one in which I called the shots and rose or fell by my decisions, learning from my mistakes as I went? Not something I was ready for.

Yet existence in meth psychosis, believing my family was with the Mossad and gaslighting me, and the FBI was pulling the strings? Terrifying…but a terror I knew was survivable. Showing up to my interview with the FBI after a good night's sleep might have led to some kind of success. Success is something I'm unprepared for.

"NOW YOU'RE GOING TO BE ARRESTED," Boolean Agent Denton says.

It's just a Boolean Operator, I tell myself. Agent Denton sits

Thirteen: The Interview

across from me, wearing a blue-and-white striped short-sleeve dress shirt. Friendly, professional, asking me cursory questions about Bangkok, about Omar. His partner sits to my left, at the head of the interview table. He wears a mustache and a grey Members Only jacket. Looking like a hard-charging private detective from an early eighties' TV drama.

At one point I get confused when someone shows me a picture of Suqami. "That guy sent me an email," I say, pointing at the picture. "I mean, *Omar* sent me an email." It's an honest mistake—the agents don't pursue any subsequent line of questioning. Despite the meth and the Boolean Agent Denton, I stay calm. *You have nothing to hide. You are telling the truth.* The interview lasts maybe twenty minutes. There's no tape recorder, no good-cop-bad-cop action.

But the interview goes quite badly for me.

Agent Denton offers no revelations about the Boolean Operators.

He doesn't explain the years of gaslighting. Says nothing of the vast counterterrorism war-game with me at its nexus. I fully expect the agents to tell me yes, I have been part of an FBI operation. I want to feel validated, a part of something greater than myself that helped others. Instead, I feel like what I've felt like going back twenty years: a failure.

Of course, if I hadn't partied on meth the night before?

Who knows how it all might've gone.

July 28, 2005. I wake up on the floor of a cell. This time it isn't a holding tank. I have my own suite, as it were. I'd have been better off in the holding tank.

The "safety cell" has padded walls and contains one naked prisoner…me. For warmth and covering, I have a straitjacket and a furniture-moving blanket.

"Someone's gonna bang on the door," a sheriff's deputy told me after they held me down, stripped my clothes away, and locked me inside. "You make some sign you're alive."

I guess I would've treated those deputies the same if our roles were reversed.

The day before, Aunt Koral's housekeeper, Fauna, called the cops on me. Completely inappropriate, of course. If you're gonna bother the police every time someone tries to break in and steal valuables to pawn for meth money… The day before that, I *had* broken in. Stolen the Tiffany clock, the gift to my Uncle Jupiter from my mom and Aunt Anne.

The pawnbroker's forty dollars were gone to meth by the next morning.

When Fauna called the cops, I was trying a repeat performance. The police showed up when I was on the porch, fumbling at the back-door lock. Good luck: you hear about dudes going into homes where they aren't welcome and getting slapped with home invasion charges. A serious beef.

Me, I'm arrested for failure to appear in court on my previous case. It should've been no more than an overnight trip to jail. But I refused to cooperate with police, demanding they call FBI Agent Denton. Cops love this. Spending their time on college-educated guys who break into their relatives' upper-class homes to steal for meth money. Then demand the FBI be called in. There's probably a study somewhere indicating this is the reason most men and women pursue careers in law enforcement.

Thirteen: The Interview

Criminal mastermind I am, I have the pawn shop receipt for stolen Tiffany clock in my wallet when they arrest me.

How does one cope with something like being stripped naked by several sheriff's deputies and held in a safety cell? First off: Today I am well aware of the fact many, many people have coped with far worse circumstances than ever befell me. At the time, huddled under my straitjacket-blanket? I just sort of figure, *this is my lot in life.* I don't have the tools to conduct an intensive search of the safety cell, which would've uncovered the person responsible for my presence there (I was alone).

I cannot understand my choices led to my situation…

At the time—and even for years afterwards—I blame those sheriff's deputies…

I blame myself.

Eventually I learn to focus not on how my mistakes weakened me…

But rather on using my experiences as sources of strength.

Strength comes from forgiveness…like Gandhi said: *The weak can never forgive. Forgiveness is the attribute of the strong.*

Today, I forgive myself for putting myself and those deputies in the positions I did.

I can *choose to believe* the deputies had compassion for me in their hearts…

Whereas had our roles been reversed? I *know* what would've been in my heart.

(It wouldn't have been compassion.)

Of course, these insights don't come for years. In the safety cell, a certain type of detachment. A turtle in its shell. Buffeted by the outside world, *feeling that world*, while not truly interacting with it. Hanging on, hoping the world changes, or goes away entirely. As a kid, the best way to endure the bullying was to do nothing until the bullies left.

"DON'T WORRY," a Boolean sheriff's deputy tells me. "WE'LL THROW YOUR PAPERWORK AWAY. YOU'LL BE OUT OF HERE IN NO TIME."

Boolean Agent Denton: "I'M ON MY WAY. WE'LL SPRING YOU LOOSE."

After I spend around twenty-four hours naked in the padded safety cell, a sheriff's deputy unlocks the door, plants a folded orange sweatsuit on the floor, instructs me to get dressed. No dice! I remain steadfast: No cooperation until FBI Agent Denton is brought onto the case. Soon enough, there are more sheriff's deputies…many more…they pin me down and force me into the jail orange. Bound in leg shackles and belly chain, I'm transported to the locked psychiatric ward at San Francisco General Hospital. Two years after my Uncle Jupiter and my old college friends tried to have me committed (or so I believe they did), I end up committed.

Two years. About as long as it takes to earn an associate degree.

A few days in the locked ward at SF General: shaving in a bucket of cold water, participating in an arts-and-crafts session led by a kind woman, a volunteer donating her time to help us psych ward patients/inmates. I have a private room…a nice man brings me cookies before lights out.

All on the taxpayer's bill.

On your bill.

The next day, a burly doctor with a thick reddish beard enters my room. A female nurse stands off to the side.

Thirteen: The Interview

"Take a seat!" the doctor barks.

"I prefer to stand." I'm in my hospital gown, my hands folded in front of me. I don't have to force myself to be calm. With the threat of physical violence, comes an almost eerie composure. Maybe because I've had almost no experience with actual violence.

"Take a seat." The doctor's voice is barely below a shout. He's probably frightened. I would be if I were him. I'm a head taller than him; he can't know I won't be violent. He's just some guy trying to get through a shift. "We called Agent Denton," he says, resigned to the fact his patient will remain standing. "He's out of the country. You'll have to get into the jail orange."

"I'm not cooperating until I talk to Agent Denton."

"He's out of the country!" the nurse yells. Now I am starting to get frightened, as the staff starts to lose their cool. It's a short-lived relief when the doctor and nurse leave: Soon enough, a team of sheriff's deputies, led by a female captain, crash into my room. They pin me down with padded riot shields, strip me naked, and force me into the orange sweatsuit. I'm not particularly frightened…it's all part of the normal routine of my life, going back to when that cop searched my apartment after the domestic violence call.

From the psych ward, it's back to County Jail. More belly chains and leg shackles. It will be my second and next-to-final incarceration. It's been just over two years since I started hearing the Boolean Operators, and a year since starting to believe the FBI is behind it.

I don't want to break free from the psychosis…
I don't believe I am in psychosis.

There's something different about me and my life, that's for sure.

It isn't concern about hearing voices and hallucinating…

It's the frustration…

Human beings, not something in my mind, are responsible.

My family knows about it. I'm sure of it. If your loved one is in drug psychosis, one problem you may face is *she or he thinks you're responsible.* It's a serious problem. Your loved one *believes* you are talking to her or him through the walls and from the invisible stealth bombers. For us as addicts, maybe it's a way to maintain connections to others while at the same time driving them away. Psychosis may substitute for those bonds with you, which we don't feel capable of making.

While I'm hearing Boolean versions of people, it's like those people are still in my life.

I spend a week or so in jail. The Boolean Operators are there with me, of course.

"YOUR FBI MISSION IS TO EXPOSE YOUR FAMILY'S SPYING!"

Uncle Jupiter picks me up after I'm released. "Someday, kiddo, we'll talk about the meth," he says, as he drives me to Lynn's apartment, where Mickey is staying. "Why you're protecting your drug dealer." While it's not entirely clear what he means, he can't be faulted for his belief: Removing the drugs (in the form of the dealer), will remove the problem.

"YOU ARE A MOSSAD SPY! YOU ARE A MOSSAD SPY!" The Booleans are screaming at him. The Booleans are so loud: *I cannot believe* Uncle Jupiter can't hear them.

Mickey and I return to our studio on Denslowe Drive.

Thirteen: The Interview

Nights holding him tight in my arms, crying, huddled on the foam-rubber mattress we share as a bed. The thumping of the FBI helicopter blades outside, Boolean Bob Mueller assuring me the agents will kick down the door any minute. I keep Mickey on his leash even inside our studio so the FBI agents won't hurt him when he tries to defend me and our home.

After my trip to the psychiatric ward, my parents cut me off. No more rent, allowance, or groceries. They'll pay for rehab, nothing else.

There's no other choice but the Ohlhoff House.

First day in rehab. Mickey has gone to live with Victoria G. out in Fairfield. She is an angel of a woman, who responds to my Craigslist posting about a foster home. Thurston, a contractor in his mid-fifties, shows me to my bed. Thurston put his house and marriage into a crack pipe and smoked them. His insurance provides one last chance in rehab. I follow him up a twisting narrow stairway to the third-floor dormitory. The dorm is a massive open room, divided into little sections by falling-apart dressers and armoires. Each section has two beds. Thurston shows me to a bed near a window that offers a view of the San Francisco downtown skyline. The same view as my college dormitory room with Logan.

"Here you go." Thurston takes a pack of cigarettes from the pocket of his flannel shirt. "Luxury accommodations. You got a cell phone, some way to stay in touch?"

I shake my head. "I lost it."

He shrugs, heads downstairs to smoke.

I'm staring at the Transamerica Pyramid when there's a tap

on my shoulder. "You've got my old bed," says the gentleman who introduces himself. "I'm moving into a sober living house." He shakes my hand. "Good luck to you," he says, a genuine expression of goodwill.

I'll never see him again. Later, Thurston will tell me: "That guy you met, he was in a band called _____."

I've heard of the band, of course. It was so famous, I can almost guarantee you've heard of it, too.

Another resident was Major League Baseball's Most Valuable Player. Very well-known in his playing days. We'll get to be friends in the months to come. He brings food home from work and offers it to me. It won't be until I leave rehab I'll realize: The food he offers me, always has turkey—turkey soup, turkey quesadillas, turkey quiche. I chuckle to myself, thinking I was the butt of a pro ballplayer hazing routine: "You are what you eat."

My first night in the Ohlhoff House, a band called *Bread & Roses* sets up in the living room and plays for us. I sit off to the side, reading a book about the National Security Agency.

I don't want to be here…

These people aren't like me…

Typical rehab ideas. Offended, having to be around people who, because of their addiction, are so similar to me. *The one you hate most is the one who's most like you*, one of my sponsors will teach me one day.

"YET SUCH IS THE LOT OF A PERSON SO DEEPLY IMMESHED IN THE FBI," the Booleans say. I've stopped wondering whether they will ever go away. They are as much a part of my life as my hands and feet. Anyway, when I'm not

Thirteen: The Interview

using meth, the voices don't bother me much…

The paranoia. That's the problem.

Still believing conspiracies. I'll be sent to prison for life, accused of helping the terrorists, made the fall guy in a vast coverup. I've let down the FBI, been a failure in my trainee role. Never sure which paranoia is worse. I'm like a frightened pet, never sure when his master will lash out in retribution for some perceived slight.

Uncle Jupiter shows up for the Ohlhoff House version of Thanksgiving dinner, a few days before the actual holiday. "Koral couldn't make it," he says. Our turkey and potatoes are brought from the kitchen. It's an Ohlhoff Thanksgiving tradition; the counselors and administrators do the serving.

"Watch out for the water," I tell Uncle Jupiter, after a counselor pours our glasses. "It's not filtered. The other night, I found a minnow swimming in mine."

Jupiter smiles, all teeth and goodwill. He is Mark Burnsen, is Victor, is Logan. It feels like I felt sitting at the Thanksgiving table at the Karnmanee Palace Hotel. About to embark on an adventure I should've steered in a different direction.

When I was sixteen and living with Uncle Jupiter for the summer, I once waited for a bus on Geary Boulevard. Jupiter happened to be driving by on his way to the ballpark. He saw me, shouted from his Mercedes. I ran across lanes of traffic to where he'd pulled over in a bus stop. At the ballpark, we ate peanuts, dropping shells until the concrete was littered with husks. Uncle Jupiter never left the park until the final out was recorded. No matter how hopeless the score, or how the San

Francisco wind howled across the Candlestick Park bleachers.

"What are you up to?" he asks me as the Ohlhoff House counselor sets down a bowl of gravy.

I know what it means: *Do I have a job?*

This time? I have an answer I think he'll like.

"Stanford University," I say. "I'm working in their new Cancer Center." Stanford hired me to write summaries of how volunteer subjects of proposed clinical trials will be protected from unnecessary risk. My summaries go to Stanford's Institutional Review Board, which modifies and/or approves the trials. From there, hopefully the drug companies make better medicines. Sometimes it works; sometimes it seems like all they do is waste tens of millions of dollars.

Uncle Jupiter cuts a piece of turkey and spears it with his fork. "When will you get a promotion?"

I move a piece of tomato around my plate. Uncle Jupiter is simply doing the best he knows how. He's encouraging me to work harder at a goal—promotion through Stanford University—that doesn't mean much to me. But he—like so many others in my family—is no more qualified to help me with my problems than if I had a blocked artery and asked him to perform open heart surgery.

"I started meditating," I say, changing the subject.

"Will meditating put food on the table?"

"Once a month we go serve food to the homeless."

"Do they pay you?"

"Maybe the Universe pays us."

I'm trying to be lighthearted, making a joke. Remembering the good times with Uncle Jupiter, when we could laugh together. But Uncle Jupiter's having none of it. "You gotta eat," he says, reaching across the table for a bread roll.

It's my own fault. Why should I expect my Uncle Jupiter to respect me for living up to my own standards, instead of trying to conform to his? I never lived up to my own standards. I've dreamed all along about becoming a writer. Am still a person who feels the world needs to change to suit me. Later, I introduce my uncle to the baseball MVP...they talk about golf, and both seem happy to have met.

The Ohlhoff House has educational classes on Saturday mornings. A nurse comes to talk about STDs. "I know it sounds weird," he says, holding up a banana and a condom. "Last time a guy admitted he didn't know how to use a condom." As I, a guy who won MVP for Major League Baseball, and twenty or so other adult male residents look on, the nurse unwraps the condom and rolls it onto the banana.

Forget Thanksgiving dinner. I should've invited Uncle Jupiter to see this.

"NO LESSON IS TOO OBSCURE!"

In rehab the days pass slowly; the months pass quickly. Weekdays I wake at four in the morning. The train gets me to Stanford and back in time for the 6:00 p.m. dinner bell. My job goes along in the usual ways...the college education I was provided allows me to get by without too much effort.

Soon, rehab isn't good enough for me any more...

More sense of entitlement. I stop engaging with the other residents, start arguing with my process group counselor. *I work for Stanford University. What am I doing living with a bunch of drug addicts?* Stanford owns an apartment complex off campus. I sign a lease on a one-bedroom at 211 Swain Way. It's too much money; half my paycheck goes right back to Stanford for rent. No wonder their graduates go on to earn millions. It doesn't matter. I have what I think I want...Victoria G. in Fairfield has taken exceptional care of Mickey and returned him to me. I have the apartment, job, etc.

Yet deep down I still feel like a failure.

I'm writing for Stanford—my clinical trial summaries, a newsletter for the Cancer Center—but I'm not *really* a writer... at least, not the kind I want to be. I want to write something meaningful; want to put myself out there on the page.

In December 2005, at a Stanford holiday party, I sit across from a friendly, bearded professor-type who holds about twelve degrees and had discovered a new form of plankton. When he mentions his plan to amble over to the bar for a glass of wine and asks, "Would you like me to bring you one?" I say yes. I cut myself off after one glass. Two, at most.

One of the first things you notice when the FBI arrests you? How comfortable the handcuffs are. They're made of molded plastic. Don't cut into your wrists like regular cop handcuffs. It's April 2006. Three years after the Boolean Operators arrived to help me make havoc of my life. I'm in the lobby of the FBI Field Office.

Again.

I'd been many times before. To drop off "evidence" of the conspiracies against me. Asking to speak with the Duty Agent, submitting written requests I be formally informed of the

Thirteen: The Interview

ongoing FBI intercession in my affairs.

This time, I'm at the FBI offices because Stanford has fired me. Some arcane Ivy-League-of-the-West tradition, about how employees are supposed to *show up for work*. Instead of smoking meth at home and not answering the phone (I went back to meth soon after those holiday party glasses of wine). After my termination, I did the natural thing. Began lodging complaints with the FBI over improper conduct of clinical trials at Stanford.

There are other drains on my resources…

A doctored picture of me appeared in the 2006 *Sports Illustrated* Swimsuit Issue. On page 222. Sure, the caption named the man as Peter Butler, hairstylist for the swimsuit models. But it was me, all right. With a devil's ear and bat-wing tattoo, my hands curled as if masturbating, a phallic symbol in the map positioned above me. "My" foot is positioned so as to appear in a model's crotch. The model was supposed to be Poem. Her hand is positioned so as to appear curled around the trunk of a potted tree, another phallic symbol. The picture is supposed to have been taken in the Bahamas, where Satam al Suqami travelled in May 19, 2000, in order to re-enter the United States and extend his legal length of stay here.

Sports Illustrated Swimsuit Issue 2006, page 222

"THE FBI IS SENDING YOU A MESSAGE," the Booleans say. "THEY ARE POWERFUL ENOUGH TO PUT A PHOTOGRAPH OF YOU IN ONE OF THE WORLD'S MOST POPULAR MAGAZINE ISSUES."

Indeed. We're past the ambiguous nature of the article on HyperSonic Sound in the *New York Times Magazine*. Well... it must be part of my FBI training. Or a global criminal conspiracy the FBI needs to made aware of. My complaint against Stanford was legitimate (in my mind), and it was entangled with greater, more far-reaching concerns. Omar from Bangkok, 9/11 conspiracies.

"FULFILLING YOUR OWN ROLE AS A TOP-SECRET OPERATIVE!"

I'd taken the train from Palo Alto. A delay as the tracks closed so fire engines could race to a burning building. At the FBI offices, I'd handed my driver's license to the receptionist behind bullet-proof glass. She asked me to wait. I took a seat in a comfortable armchair.

"Can I see that license again?" The receptionist asked.

I'm not the most street-smart person, if you haven't guessed. I should've known something was up when the FBI receptionist asked to see my license the second time.

But I simply kept waiting. Until soon enough, I got my wish...

I got my chance to speak with an FBI agent.

"You have a warrant out for your arrest," the agent informs me as she put the cuffs on. "Failure to appear at a court hearing. We had to check."

Of course. I was supposed to have shown up to see the judge on my previous case.

Thirteen: The Interview

After the FBI arrests me, uniformed officers from the Department of Homeland Security escort me to a holding cell in the basement of the Federal Building. I know enough to be polite when they ask questions. Even the standard one-two of "What is your date of birth?" followed by "How old are you?" I guess cops ask this to catch you if you're lying or are under the influence.

The FBI arrested me for an outstanding bench warrant, yes. But in a larger sense, my arrest was for failing to serve my communities. I could've appeared before the judge on my previous case—like I'd promised—and completed my probation, paid my debt to society. I could've remained clean off meth, and thus stayed working for Stanford...received a free Stanford education as part of my employment. Used it to bring some measure of good to others.

Instead, I chose to try and solve grandiose conspiracies, and hold fast to my resentments and false beliefs. I chose to keep taking from my communities, until my communities could take no more.

The DHS cuts me loose. Maybe because before I'd left my Stanford apartment that morning for the FBI office, I'd thought to dress well and have money in my pocket. And because of my being polite and respectful to the DHS officers. Or maybe a call came in from the top levels of U.S. Intelligence: *He's too important to us. We need him out on the streets.* For whatever reasons, an hour or two after the FBI arrests me, my soles slap the pavement outside the Federal Building.

"HE'S ON THE STREETS! THEY CUT HIM LOOSE, AND HE'S FREE!" The Boolean Operators sing. Thoughts of my family are gone. I take the train back to Stanford.

But not before hooking up with my meth connect.

The following month—May 2006—I'll once again wake up on the floor. Of a homeless shelter in San Francisco. Mickey is gone forever. Victoria G., bless her heart, has taken him to live on the East Coast. I like to picture him running alongside her young son, through a sunlit glade. Bringing joy into a boy's heart, the way he did for me.

Even today—certainly past the end of Mickey's natural lifetime—days pass when I don't think about Uncle Jupiter, Aunt Koral, or my parents. When I don't wish I could go back and never take that first drink from a champagne flute at my aunt's wedding. But not one day goes by when I don't think about that wonderful mutt Mickey and all the love he was capable of bringing.

Later that day, at the homeless shelter, I'm sitting in the outdoor area where smoking is permitted. A guy goes around selling cigarettes for a quarter. I have two quarters in my pocket. I call the man over. Later, as I'm smoking, I realize: *I just spent one-half of my entire net worth on a single cigarette.*

And it seems clear: *The FBI is not going to take me seriously if I keep at the meth.*

The meth has cost me a career at Stanford, considered by many to be among the top institutes of learning in the world.

It cost me Mickey, the living being I love most…

That night, I sleep on a foam-rubber mattress on the shelter floor.

The next day, I go to see about checking back in to the Ohlhoff House.

Fourteen:
Sebastian

My sponsor asked that I merely remain open-minded to the possibility that there was a Power greater than myself, one of my own understanding.

—from the "Big Book" of
Alcoholics Anonymous

Sebastian might as well be a Viking of legend. At the prow of a ship, holding fast to the mast as a storm lashes fury. He's the speaker at the regular seven o'clock Sunday night AA meeting. Hosted by your faithful residents of the Henry Ohlhoff House.
  (Me included.)
  Every Sunday after six we struggle up from fading living room couches and armchairs. Some of us are on restriction—within our first couple weeks in rehab and confined to the House. Have spent the day watching television, in and out of sleep. Desperate for an end to the nerve-jangling and cravings for booze/intoxicants. Sometimes wishes come true. A well-worn logbook sits on the coffee table. Any resident can write his (the Ohlhoff House is a men's residence) thoughts, feelings, challenges, or—yes—accomplishments. Trevor got a job. Scott celebrated a week clean. Etcetera.

> "WE WISH TO WRITE SOMETHING TOO! YET WE ARE ONLY VOICES, LACKING THE NECESSARY MATERIAL FORM TO OPERATE A PEN."

The pendulum clock ticks towards seven. We rearrange the dining room furniture, carving out space for the other alcoholics and addicts who will visit our temporary home to spend an hour with us. A resident brews a pot of coffee, another puts out Chips Ahoy and Fig Newtons.

The meeting starts. Sebastian's face is smooth; his biceps show under a black dry-fit workout shirt. In a heavy Brooklyn accent, he's self-reflective and matter-of-fact, telling his story of having worked at one of the biggest financial firms…

Then being a crack addict, living on the streets, abandoning his infant daughter.

As Sebastian speaks, meeting-goers in the back of the room start a side conversation. If I were Sebastian, I'd be leaping over the speaker's table. Fists pinwheeling, out to crack heads. Sebastian looks calm, ignores the side-talkers, continues his story.

I remember long-ago Sunday nights. Lying in bed, struggling towards the first sleep in forty hours. Another Monday at the Biotech Giant looming. *Next weekend I'll start writing my book.* The meth high dulled to a quavering twang, depression setting in, desperate for the party to keep going. Anything to not wake up the next Monday morning, being me again. The only solace: knowing it was just a matter of steeling myself for a few days at the office. Until the following Saturday, after a workout at Cheetah's, and the start of another binge. No problem can't be put aside for five days.

FOURTEEN: SEBASTIAN

Sebastian wraps up his share.
He is confident.
He's spent nights with prostitutes and cocaine in his palatial condo. It, along with everything else, drawn into a glass pipe, became swirling crack-mist. Yet I picture him rising for work tomorrow, happy with who he is and what he can bring to the world.
I want to be like him. I want what he's got.
I shift my weight back and forth, standing on the fringes of the post-meeting group gathered around Sebastian. Like we inmates gathered around Deputy Horne's baseball card, or kids around Corey Hillman in the Oakmont cafeteria. "I want to talk to this man right here," Sebastian says, pointing at me as he excuses himself from a conversation. "How ya doing?" We shake hands.

I shrug. "I've been sober a couple of months." Says it all.

"You're staying upstairs?"

"Yeah."

He nods, studies me.

"Sebastian…I'm, ah…looking for a sponsor."

A few nights later, my new sponsor and I meet in a back room of the Ohlhoff House. Sebastian sits close at my left side, like he's driving. Close enough to touch if I reach out my hand. Closer than Omar, ahead of me on the Bangkok streets. "Tell me your story," he says, encouraging me to launch into my life's history. At one point, he interrupts my rambling tale by saying, "I feel like I'm listening to my own story." He's patient, laughs at my stupid jokes, ignores my egotistical theories.

"So," he says, "you got a job?"

"The Online Collaborative Oncology Group."

Sebastian chuckles. "The what?"

"Biotech company. Downtown." After moving back into the Ohlhoff House, I'd held down a temp job in a Dean's Office of the University of California, San Francisco. Nice co-workers. Unbearable tedium. Booking conference rooms, eight hours a day. There'd been a Craigslist ad, an outfit called OCOG. I sent a resume, got called for the interview. Told the Dean's Office I had a dentist appointment.

Jonathon Fendelman, OCOG's General Manager, interviewed me in his office. "I see you worked at Stanford." He studied my resume. "Only a couple months, though. Was that just a contract that came to an end?"

"Yes," I lied. "A contract that came to an end." I lied to my UCSF managers after Jonathon offered me the job. Told the Dean's Office I'd stay on for another couple weeks. Then sent them an email on a Saturday, informing them I wouldn't be back on Monday.

"OCOG sent me to Stockton," I tell Sebastian, in the back room of the Ohlhoff House. "I spent the day there yesterday."

"What's Stockton, east?"

"Yeah. Jessica—she works with me, was like my mentor—picked me up in Oakland, at the BART station. We drove… to a hospital…a medical center, or something."

"Uh-huh."

Silence, except for the three lanes of traffic cruising Oak Street. I think about Omar…

"INCHES FROM SPEEDING HUNKS OF STEEL AND CHURNING FUEL!"

FOURTEEN: SEBASTIAN

Sebastian looks thoughtful for a moment. "What did you do?"

"Nothing."

"You'd think you did something."

I shrug. "I can't figure it out."

"Maybe they're hoping you'll mature into a role."

"Yeah," I say. "It's not really what I'm cut out for. I sat in a back room with sorted through piles of papers. You know, medical charts."

"Like, forms?"

"Uh, yeah." I feel a yawn coming, stifle it, crack my knuckles. "We compared the numbers to other forms. Made sure they matched."

"What if they don't match?"

"You fill out another form."

It gets the type of quiet you can feel the earth spin.

"They asked me to go to Texas," I say.

"Who, OCOG?"

"Yeah...guess they have their sights on me, moving up."

"Texas, huh?" Sebastian taps his pen against his knee, chews his lip.

"The thing is," I lean forward in my chair, "I *have to go on this trip*. If I want to make a good impression. But the Ohlhoff House might not let me." In fact, I've been stressed out for days. Worried about how to make Texas happen, despite the Ohlhoff House objections. Sebastian sits patient through my usual litany of complaints...rehab rules, counselors, etc.

"Texas," he says in his Brooklyn accent. "I mean, that could be a real disaster. What if you tried to score meth there?"

"Score meth...on a business trip? I've gone on plenty of trips, never tried to score meth." The Biotech Giant sent me places: Montreal, Nashville, Vancouver, and Manchester, England.

"That was different, dude. I mean, look where you are now." I feel the bile rising. How dare Sebastian suggest I—having arrived in rehab from a homeless shelter after losing everything to meth—might try and score meth?

I grudgingly concede the point to Sebastian. The next day, Jonathon Fendelman tells me the trip to Texas is off.

Sebastian meets me in Noe Valley, a coffee shop there. He has new reading glasses that fold like spiders' legs. They keep collapsing when he extracts them from their case. He heaves them aside, frustrated. "I got you a present," he says. I examine it: A copy of the "Big Book" of Alcoholics Anonymous.

"You wanna do some reading?" he says, opening his own Big Book. The pages have more fluorescent highlighter ink than white space.

"Couldn't I do that later? I mean, we're together; shouldn't we be talking, not reading?"

"We read out loud."

"Out loud? Like in elementary school?"

"I thought your lips moved when you read anyway. Don't worry."

"WE ARE HAPPY TO LISTEN TO YOU READ."

We take turns reading. A paragraph or two out loud. Then discussing. At first, I'm self-conscious. Everyone will overhear. The coffee shop is filled with some of San Francisco's elite. Noe Valley-dwellers with perfect skin and clothes, young mothers and fathers shifting past our table. They'll know I'm

FOURTEEN: SEBASTIAN

a drug addict.

But I'm with Sebastian…

I feel like I did hanging out with Mark Burnsen, Victor, Logan, Omar.

On the other side of the plate-glass windows, the sky over Noe Valley grows dark. On this same street I made my decision to score meth the night before my FBI interview.

Sebastian and I read the story of Bill Wilson. AA's co-founder. His earliest memories of feeling heroic, discovering liquor in the midst of excitement around him. Imagining a future of greatness for himself. Wilson describes all this on the *first page*. I remember the porno movie downstairs from my aunt's wedding reception, the German bier-fest. *These kids actually* like *me*. Sebastian has me read from page twelve. Bill Wilson gets "…convinced that God is concerned with us humans…when we humans want God enough."

Sebastian sets his Big Book down. "Do you have a concept of God?"

"I dunno. I'm Jewish, technically."

"Technically?"

"My mom is Jewish…I didn't even know I was, growing up. We had Christmas trees. When I moved out here, my Uncle Jupiter's family was Jewish…I started realizing I might be, too."

"Your who?"

"No one," I say. "My uncle."

Sebastian nods. "Do you pray?" he asks.

I shake my head.

He says: "Well, here's a suggestion. Start praying. It doesn't matter if you believe in God or not. Can you do that?"

I shrug. "Pray for what?"

"Whatever you want."

As he helps me adopt spirituality, Sebastian makes something clear. "You're helping me, too," he says. "This is how I stay sober. Passing along what my sponsors gave me." Thus, I don't have to be suspicious of Sebastian's motives. It's like the patient-therapist relationship: The trade-off is clear; the stated motives aren't in question.

Sure, I believe Sebastian is connected to the FBI. Everyone in my life is. I assume Sebastian updates the Bureau on my progress, strategizes in secret with agents. It doesn't matter; Sebastian's essential motivation is to be my sponsor.

Sebastian has empathy for me.

Empathy is a desirable human quality.

He has other desirable human qualities, too…

The more desirable human qualities we have, the more others want to be like us.

This, I have found, is the defining characteristic of those who best helped me out of addiction.

Sebastian—and others like him—led me from the darkness when they gave me hope I could become a worthwhile human, too. It's not wrong to strive to attain things: money, status, power. But as an addict, I'm not likely to respect you because you've attained *things*. Addiction's great irony: we addicts are good at getting things. The daily struggle to feed my meth habit took at least as much effort as that I put forth to succeed at the Biotech Giant. More, in fact.

As an addict, I'm more likely to respect you if you strive to lead the type of life I'd long wished to lead, yet fallen short.

Fourteen: Sebastian

A spiritual life of serving a higher purpose, helping others, self-improvement.

Even before meeting Sebastian, life in the Ohlhoff House opened my mind to a possibility: I could go a single day without booze or drugs. To the average person, it seems preposterous to even consider whether this might be true. But to an addict like me, to voluntarily go a single day without drugs or booze? Like sending a human being to the moon.

"WE HAVE CERTAIN MOON LANDING CONSPIRACIES TO BUY INTO AS WELL!"

Through Sebastian, I begin to learn: With spirituality—the constant search for a loving presence who cares about *me*—a day spent without booze or drugs may even be worthwhile.

"*I hope you get back on track…*" *The way Officer Pagano says it makes me realize she cares about me…insofar as she cares about human beings in general, and I—even if just barely—fit into that category.*

My sixty-day jail stretch imparted one important lesson. I didn't do drugs when I was locked up (exception: I snorted two lines of chopped-up codeine one afternoon). Because I didn't have the *jail skills* to score drugs. Like my fellow inmates did. If my objective is to *quit doing drugs*, the answer is simple: voluntarily incarcerate myself for the rest of my life.

"BUT THAT MAKES NO SENSE!"

Sebastian teaches me the objective is *not* to quit drinking and drugs. Quitting is a means to an end. My objective is to find a way to *learn to live sober*. Spirituality gets me from a chief life's accomplishment of writing thirty pages of a Hunter Thompson ripoff, to applying myself towards becoming a writer.

Sebastian has the top down in his convertible; the night is unseasonably warm. We're coming from an AA meeting. He drops me off in front of the Ohlhoff House.

"Work on your fourth step," he says as the Ohlhoff's gothic spires loom. "Your moral inventory…what you want to keep, not just what you have to let go."

As I open the car door, it almost hits a woman going along the sidewalk.

"Excuse me," I say. She's carrying a long tube, like for a yoga mat. Or a sniper's rifle. As I climb the steps to the ancient Victorian, I hear Sebastian call to her. When I turn to look, she's leaning into his car. At the top of the steps, I sit and light a cigarette. The woman climbs into Sebastian's car. They drive off.

It's not the type of scenario that leaves one with the sensation something incredibly *good* is gonna come from it.

Sure enough, Sebastian doesn't show up for our next sponsor meeting.

Or the one after that.

Won't answer his phone, either. "Sebastian," I leave a message, "you gotta decide. Do you want to be my sponsor, or not?"

His return call comes when I'm in process group; my phone turned off as per the rules. "I'm struggling," Sebastian's recorded voice says. "I'm in active addiction." The woman he met took him to a hotel room, scored drugs. You know the rest. Sebastian leaves some good things behind. A young daughter, a job, his 12-step community.

"A SPONSEE WHO OPERATES AT THE HIGHEST LEVEL OF TOP-SECRET COUNTERTERRORISM WORK!"

Fourteen: Sebastian

Downstairs, my counselor Mitch is still around. Mitch is the kind of gem you unearth if you spend any amount of time around the recovery community. He drank until his liver threw in the towel. Got sober, and a liver transplant. How many dudes do you find walking around with *a whole new organ,* after toxifying their last one into worthlessness?

Mitch balances his notebook on his knee, pats the pocket of his flannel shirt. A leftover tic from when he'd reach for a cigarette. He used to get his cigarettes in soft packs and open them from the bottom. So, when someone asked to bum a smoke, he could show them the top of the pack. Claiming it was brand-new and he didn't want to open it.

"Mitch...you know Sebastian, my sponsor?"

"Yeah, sure. How's he doing?"

"Less than exemplary." I give Mitch the bad news. "What should I do...go look for him?"

"Sebastian knows what to do." Mitch says. "He'll find his way back, when he's ready."

Without Sebastian, my pursuit of spirituality drifts.

At my desk in the OCOG offices, I aimlessly flip through the pages of a clinical trial protocol. The words, figures, and tables...all incomprehensible.

The picture of me on page 222 of the 2006 *Sports Illustrated* Swimsuit Issue?

"THERE'S SOMETHING WE CAN SINK OUR TEETH INTO! IF ONLY WE HAD TEETH."

I fantasize about dropping meth in my coffee mug sitting on my Steelcase desk. Skipping over to one of the high-rise hotels across Market Street. Renting a room, filling the bathtub with ice and booze. Calling a meth connect and heading to the North Beach strip clubs.

OCOG terminates my contract a couple weeks later. Maybe they discovered I was fired from Stanford, had lied in my interview. There was the time Jonathon Fendelman found me sleeping in a conference room. Years down the road, Jonathon will be a major source of support, going out of his way to help me with my resume and job search after I get clean.

I file for unemployment insurance.

Nine-hundred-dollar checks begin to arrive at the Ohlhoff House. One every two weeks.

Walter, a fellow resident, works out every morning at the Bay Club. A high-end health club in North Beach. I start catching rides with him. We entertain each other—talking in funny voices, making up characters, poking fun at the Ohlhoff House. I spend the days swimming laps in the Bay Club's heated pool, hitting tennis balls on the roof. There's an AstroTurf surface and a ball machine.

"YOU ARE DOING SO WELL AT YOUR REHAB ENDEAVORS!"

The Boolean Operators are friendly.

My thoughts are not.

The FBI will stop at nothing to prevent the world from knowing Satam al Suqami was an infiltrator. They'll pin 9/11 on me...will assassinate me.

Depression...the FBI hates me, for failing in my role.

The FBI believes I had something to do with helping the terrorists.

Anxiety...I'm selling out my fellow Americans...they have the right to know about Omar.

Fourteen: Sebastian

It's all selfish, self-centered fear. Even my concerns about Americans' right to know are mostly due to my wanting to be liked. I lack initiative…I'm sitting around waiting for the FBI to show up and wrap matters into a nice conclusion, just for me.

"IT SHOULD HAPPEN ANY DAY NOW!"

From the roof of the Bay Club, one can almost see the North Beach strip clubs where I'd partied with beautiful entertainers. Fighting the Boolean Operators, when they were master criminals threatening innocent victims everywhere. When my Boolean FBI handlers placed the highest value on my services, managing my activities with hypnosis and subliminal messaging. Back then, I was convinced, in my twisted way, I could hold my head high.

The ball machine fires another shot.

Dawn breaks over North Beach as I suck another hit from the meth pipe. I've taken up residence in a single-room-occupancy hotel. The day before, I'd still been sober. Had plans take BART to Oakland and meet Logan for lunch, like we'd been doing every couple or weeks or so.

Instead I went to a meth connect's apartment.

I hadn't planned to stand up Logan.

Hadn't planned not to be at the Ohlhoff House in time for dinner.

Hadn't planned to check into the SRO, smoke meth until midnight, then take a cab to the Ohlhoff House, gather up all my belongings, and say goodbye to rehab.

I'd gone on interviews and was about to be offered a job with UCSF…

Reached senior man status at the Ohlhoff House, slept in the best bed in the house...

Was in great shape from all the working out at the Bay Club. But they are all goals.

Not a dream.

I hadn't tried to become a writer.

In my North Beach SRO, sucking from the pipe, I begin my novel. Pounding away on a turquoise Apple clamshell laptop. The window has a view of the Beat Museum, a bookstore with a life-sized picture of Jack Kerouac and Neal Cassady in the window.

I spend my nights banging out manuscript pages. Until my unemployment insurance fraud is discovered, my checks cut off.

I pawn my laptop, and my novel disappears with it.

I spend my final year on meth in that North Beach SRO.

My last few months as Reggie.

The SRO becomes a dingy meth-cave of a room. A sink in the corner where I ash my cigarettes and urinate. I haven't showered or brushed my teeth in months. Methamphetamine alchemy becomes my hobby. Mixing potions from flammable liquids in a glass ashtray, exhaling meth smoke over the mixture, hoping for a chain reaction. Electrically charging the experiment with 9-volt batteries connected by gold cufflinks stolen from my Uncle Jupiter.

For nourishment, jelly donuts and coffee from a 24-hour shop, soup kitchens, shoplifting from supermarkets.

I smoke meth and write long letters to the U.S. Department of State. Outlining terms for my taking over leadership of the free world, after the Boolean Operators convince me I am

Fourteen: Sebastian

the lost son of John Lennon and Princess Margaret. Rightful heir to the throne of the British Empire. I deliver my treaty proposals long after midnight, slipping them under the locked door of the downtown building where the State Department has an office. Until the nighttime desk clerk shouts at me to knock it off.

I smoke meth and discover a mathematical formula *proving I am an undercover FBI operative…*

When you assign each letter in my first name "Peter" a numerical value, based upon that letter's position in the alphabet, you get:

P = 16, E = 5, and so forth…thereby "Peter" is "16, 5, 20, 5, 18." The digits add up to 28 (1+6+5…=28). The digits in 28 add up to 10, the digits in 10 add up to 1.

Use the same math with my date of birth? Your result is 2.

"Peter" equals 1… *my parents decided upon my name before I was born*

My date of birth, using the same math, equals 2… *I was born, after my parents named me*

My Social Security Number—using the same formula—equals 3… *sometime after my birth, the government assigned me a Social Security Number.*

My Selective Service Number equals 4… *sometime after I was assigned a Social Security Number, I was assigned that Selective Service Number, in preparation for possible military service.*

My California driver's license number equals 5… *after my Selective Service Number, I was given that driver's license number.*

My five unique identifiers in the order they were assigned *add sequentially to 1 through 5.*

"OBVIOUSLY, HERBERT HOOVER HAD YOU GENETICALLY ENGINEERED SINCE BEFORE BIRTH!"

But it went wrong, because of my addiction, and now the Bureau wants me dead.

I smoke meth and discover…

Metal poisoning has invaded my body. I steal tiny earth magnets from Radio Shack, soak them overnight in a glass of water, and drink the water to pull the poisoning from my organs. Magnets are a source of fascination. I affix them to the lens of my small flashlight to bend and manipulate beams of light.

"THIS IS SCIENTIFICALLY POSSIBLE! YOU HAVE DISCOVERED THE WAY."

I smoke meth and discover a corresponding ratio between Marlboro cigarettes and U.S. postage stamps; a Marlboro's circumference is exactly the same as the length of a stamp. There's no question as to the conclusion: The glue in stamps must contain methamphetamine…there must be a process to wrap stamps around cigarettes and pour water through so as to extract a cocktail of meth and nicotine. So soldiers (in the old days, soldiers always carried stamps, cigarettes, and water, right?) can brew up energy and pain relief on the battlefield. I construct a miniature distillery on the collapsing pressboard dresser next to my ashtray-alchemy. The floor of becomes littered with Marlboro filters and gloppy lumps of tobacco and stamps.

With meth, you discover all these ways the government is part of your life. How your city's architecture is a civil defense plan. That stone monument to your civic leader? Really a machine gun nest waiting to be encircled with razor wire. The pier into

Fourteen: Sebastian

the river? A ramp for amphibious vehicles to run blockades. Carry food and medical supplies to the town commons during a siege by invading armies.

I smoke meth and conduct thought experiments…

"JUST LIKE EINSTEIN!"

…aircraft carriers can be reengineered to generate power via a sodium-potassium ion exchange through a hull made of semi-permeable membrane. Same principle as the electrical mechanism of a human heart. I draft and send correspondence to the Department of Defense, explaining my findings.

Above the sink, a square of mirrored glass affixed to the wall. Next to where I've hung the picture of Poem and myself in the *Sports Illustrated* Swimsuit Issue. I stare at my reflection, picking at my face. Certain soon to catch one of the many worms tunneling beneath the dermal layer.

A meth connect arrives one night and hands me a baseball-sized package. *Felony weight.* If one of the dozens of police officers patrolling North Beach stop me as I go to drop the package to someone waiting in her parked car? As is sure to happen, eventually, if I make more of these kinds of deliveries…I won't be going away on any misdemeanor charge. Not this time.

This has been my life for the better part of a year.

When on Friday, October 19, 2007, I get dressed up in my tuxedo.

The tux is left over from a disastrous summer working as a floorwalker for the Larry Flynt's Hustler Club. Like my other employers, the Hustler Club gave me a chance, and I made them pay for it.

On my first day of work, I showed up with band-aids all over my face from where I'd picked at my skin. That morning, I'd stopped by my aunt Koral's. She happened to be cleaning out her garage.

"Look at this!" she'd said, holding up a heavy black jacket. "It's sealskin. I'm going to donate it."

That night at the Hustler Club, a call came over the walkie-talkies. "One of the owners is here," the voice said. A few minutes later, a fine-looking gentleman was standing in front of me, shaking my hand. He was wearing *a sealskin coat just like the one Koral showed me.*

I smoke meth and become convinced; my family and organized crime figures (rumors swirl about the North Beach strip clubs and organized crime; I have no proof of any connection) are setting me up to take a serious fall. After the Hustler Club rightfully fires me, I file a lawsuit against them in federal court. Not the only lawsuit I'll ever file. I hang out in the downtown law library, researching federal statues, writing briefs and sending them to various government officials. Claiming special status by some obscure act of the United States Senate.

On that October Friday, I clean my tux by setting stolen shoe polish on fire and holding the thick black sludge up to my suit. Now dressed to the nines in my tux (underneath, a light-blue shirt that looks like a pajama top), I show up for a job interview at a Larkin Street strip club. It goes about as well as you might expect. Post-interview, I slither the sidewalks. Until I find myself at the Hyatt Regency Hotel, on the Embarcadero.

In the main ballroom, a wedding reception. I consider inserting myself into the proceedings. Sauntering up to the

Fourteen: Sebastian

buffet table for a bite to eat, sidling up to the bar for a cocktail. *Blending in.* If questioned by a legitimate guest, I'll just feign ignorance. Claim I thought the celebration was for a different couple.

I stand in the entranceway.

"REMEMBER YOU ASKED US TO MARRY YOU?"

It's true…Thanksgiving Day, 2006, in my SRO hotel room, I had indeed asked the Boolean Operators to become my spouse.

"WE SAID, YES."

And now I consider myself married to the Boolean Operators. Betrothed to the disembodied voices that came to me during the pinnacle of my goal attainment, living in my home on Monterey Boulevard.

This is what I've accomplished.

In the time period of 2003 – 2004, five weddings take place.
Ten of my closest friends.
One couple asks me to be their best man.
I show up to zero of those weddings.

I'm as much a part of the Hyatt wedding as I was a part of the Brooklyn Botanical Gardens wedding twenty-three years ago. Before I followed my cousin Jess to drink champagne and watch porno movies. When the bonds between freedom and acceptance, and being intoxicated, begin to become very hard to break. Even psychosis and jail will not be enough.

"AND TODAY, WE ARE MARRIED!"

I slouch about the Hyatt hotel bar. Bottles glitter behind the polished mahogany. A towering sculpture resembles a hollowed-out globe. Terraced walkways outside the guest rooms form a pyramid, twenty stories high. It must be the greatest temporary home ever constructed! I find a half-finished drink someone left behind and slug it down.

Back in my SRO hotel, someone's left feces smeared on the seat of the common toilet. I use the bathroom down the hall.

In my room, a few hits left in my meth pipe…I smoke all that remains.

Pass out, just before midnight.

And I suppose part of me decides that part of my life is finished.

The next morning, I don my other uniform: filthy black Ben Davis slacks, a black baseball jacket with the logo of the Lake Merced Country Club (another item stolen from Uncle Jupiter), and brown Converse low-tops held together with duct tape. No socks, underwear, nothing like that. The parking lot attendant across the street lets me borrow his broom. I sweep the sidewalk in front of my hotel. Cleaning the refuse from the night before. Cigarette butts, flyers advertising the strip clubs. Hoping when I finish sweeping to the corner cafe, the owner will give me a free cup of coffee. So far, it's happened exactly once.

To my left, the Broadway Tunnel is a gaping black hole. To my right is the glittering San Francisco Bay. Just like I saw it twenty years ago, when I first arrived here from Massachusetts.

I wonder if I've got enough cell phone minutes to make a call.

Somewhere I'd heard Sebastian is sober again.

I find his number and wonder, how much time remains.

Fifteen:

Campaigns

There is a fantastic adrenaline high that comes with total involvement in almost any kind of fast-moving… campaign—especially when you're running against big odds and starting to feel like a winner.

—Hunter S. Thompson,
Fear & Loathing on the Campaign Trail '72

My fist clenches around my phone. It's Thanksgiving Day, 2007. The number 14 bus lets me off on the corner of Mission and Ocean, Excelsior District.

I've been clean a month.

I'm about to make the call to score meth.

"TODAY IS OUR WEDDING ANNIVERSARY!" the Booleans say. "DON'T FORGET."

Indeed.

Without the meth, the Boolean Operators are comforting, in their strange and twisted ways. The Boolean Operators might not even exist were it not for me! They know more about the FBI conspiracies than I do. They won't try and have me committed to any psychiatric institution. Plenty of times I've cried, thinking about what it might be like if they went away.

"SO YOU'D THINK YOU'D REMEMBER OUR ANNIVERSARY."

Yes...today, on our...*wedding anniversary*, we're on our way...*I'm on my way*...to a Thanksgiving gathering at Giles' house. Giles smoked crack and worked as a gardener for the city. He's been sober a long time now. He and his wife, Amalia, rent out bedrooms in their home to sober persons.

A month clean...may not seem like much, to me it's a miracle.

Later in the day, I'm supposed to be at Uncle Jupiter's for family dinner.

It's been seven years since I ate a Thanksgiving meal of *Pad Thai* and sticky rice in Bangkok's Karnmanee Palace Hotel.

I take my phone from my pocket, stare at the keypad.

Willing my fingers not to start pushing buttons.

A few minutes ago, my cell phone screen lit up with the number of my meth connect. I pictured him in a hotel room, hiding out, avoiding cops and bounty hunters. If he was calling to invite me to come on over and get high, watch football, drink Jack Daniels?

No. Best to let the phone ring to voicemail.

But now he's left a message.

Delete it! Without listening.

But...what if there's some problem...if he's in trouble?

The urge to use again is like a fantastic magnet, impossibly strong. My soul no more than a tiny shard of iron, trapped in an addict's body. If the voicemail message says, "Come meet me!"

...I won't have to think of *anything else...*

Except getting to his hotel room as fast as possible.

As an addict it's not so much that I think about drugs; as

that I use drugs to not think about the rest.

With drugs I won't have to think about: If I choose to believe Uncle Jupiter is disappointed in me for not succeeding in some career, it's only because he and I have different definitions of success. I know this is true! *Why won't my mind just accept it?*

Won't have to think about: A month clean—already obsessions with food and weight loss have an ironclad grip. Strangling worry about overeating turkey, calories burned and consumed.

Won't have to think about: Never became a writer. Never really tried.

"WON'T HAVE TO THINK ABOUT FORGETTING OUR ANNIVERSARY PRESENT!"

To return the meth connect's call? Means all those terrible, seemingly unsolvable problems will vanish.

In his book *The Heart of Addiction,* Lance Dodes, MD describes addiction relating to the power of making a decision. If an addict is anxious—while driving her car, say—when she steers onto the exit to her drug dealer's, rather than continues home…her anxiety disappears when she *makes her decision.* No waiting until she gets high. When she decides to use again, she *feels in control.*

If I call my meth connect from the Excelsior bus stop?

I'll feel okay *then and there.*

My unsolvable problems will go away immediately.

(Although I suppose I could pick up something for the Boolean Operators at the 24-hour Walgreens, open on holidays.)

I spend a few minutes walking those same Excelsior streets I patrolled with Mickey. Fending off conspiracies so vast they'd make your head spin. I take out my phone and look for my meth connect's number.

Then it occurs to me...

Maybe I should call Sebastian first.

"INDEED!"

Calling Sebastian is a way of making a decision, taking charge of my life.

"Hello?" Right away, Sebastian's Brooklyn accent calms my nerves. I tell him about the call from my meth connect.

"So, what's the problem?"

"Well...what if it's an emergency, and I'm the only one who can help?" Even as I'm saying it, I realize how ridiculous it sounds.

"I'll tell you what," Sebastian says. Like he's heard this kind of story a million times. "Give me your voicemail passcode. You can change it later. I'll listen to the message and call you back, let you know what's up."

"Okay," I say. "Yes. That sounds good."

I put my phone away. Above, a Perpendicular Plane appears. My FBI pursuers, working holidays. Or are they pursuers? Maybe just handlers. *You know, maybe this FBI thing isn't so bad. Maybe I really am an undercover operative.*

"YOU KNOW," the Booleans say, "THE FIRST YEAR OF MARRIAGE IS OFTEN A HONEYMOON PHASE. THEN THE REAL WORK BEGINS."

The phone rings.

"I listened to the message," Sebastian says. "It sounds like your friend might've had a couple. But he's okay. He just wanted to wish you a happy Thanksgiving."

"Thanks, Sebastian."

Fifteen: Campaigns

I hang up. Giles' and Amalia's home appears at the end of the block.

"I'm thinking about starting a blog," I tell Sebastian, sitting next to me at the Waterfront meeting. The Waterfront is a big Sunday night AA meeting in a cavernous room in a warehouse on one of the piers near North Beach.

Over the holidays, I'd had two jobs: working on a Christmas tree lot, and on a UPS truck. Very difficult to focus long enough to get through a full shift. I had to ask the UPS driver to let me off early, so I could get to an AA meeting.

I go to meetings every day, sometimes two or three a day.

I often sit in those meetings mired in resentment of what's being said, who is saying it. Judging others, bitter and angry. Yet I force myself into those meeting seats, day after day. "*If you got wasted every day,*" the meeting-goers say, "*you can go to a meeting every day.*"

"A blog, huh?" Sebastian says. "Sounds like a good idea."

"It's gonna be called *Straight Outta Rehab*. You know, 'straight' could mean, straight like not on drugs, or straight like, straightforward."

"Got it," he says, settling back into his chair.

"I need a domain name," I continue. "I have the money, but I don't have a credit card. Can you help me?"

"Sure," he says. "We can work something out."

The Waterfront secretary starts the meeting by asking if anyone is celebrating a birthday. "My name is Ed," I say when she calls on me. "I just got sixty days clean." Amid the applause, Sebastian leans over. "I'm still getting used to calling you Ed," he says.

"There are people who've known me a lot longer than you who have to remember," I say.

The idea had come one afternoon working in the Christmas tree lot. I hoisted a blue spruce cut fresh from the farm, lugged it to the roof of a Mercedes wagon, and tied it fast.

I decided…

You know what? I'm gonna start going by my middle name.

"HERE AMONGST THE TREES WE USE TO CELEBRATE THE BIRTH OF JESUS, A NEW NAME IS GIVEN TO YOU."

I'd left a message on Uncle Jupiter's answering machine. "I'm working at the Christmas tree lot." I left the address on 7th Avenue and Warren Drive. "And, just so you know, I'm starting to go by Ed." Uncle Jupiter arrived an hour later, wearing his dark blue quilted jacket he usually saved for Giants' games. He had a stack of double-chocolate-chip cookies wrapped in a napkin.

"I asked for Ed," he said, handing me a cookie. "They pointed me to you."

The first few blog entries are simple paragraphs. Written at the computer in the living room of the Ohlhoff House. I'd moved back in on Christmas Eve. "WELCOME HOME!" the Boolean Operators said as we climbed the stairs to the dormitory. "MAYBE THEY'LL GIVE US OUR OLD BED BACK."

December 25, 2007: Today marks twenty-four hours in rehab. This is the third time I've been in rehab, all three times in the same rehab. It is a nice rehab, as far as ambient surroundings and

Fifteen: Campaigns

the quality of the guys I have met, the counselors, and Program Director...all of us watch the moon rise over some buildings downtown and across the water from the top of a hill, not far from a park.

December 28, 2007: Later today I meet with my sponsor to take the "4th step" of the 12-step program of Alcoholics Anonymous. The 4th step suggests I write down the names of all the people, entities, and ideas against whom or which I harbor resentments...it is a fairly long list. Over the course of the past four years, I have been fired or summarily dismissed from eight jobs. Some I was better off without, but a couple were pretty good. Earlier this morning I typed my resume, checked the Jobs section on Craigslist, e-mailed my attorney to inquire about expungement of my criminal records.

December 31, 2007: Earlier today I visited the office of a consumer credit counselor. On the intake form I was asked to indicate my "most pressing concerns" as related to debt. I wrote, "Total debt almost $200,000, no income, poor credit, taxes not filed since 2000, no savings, no assets."

Tonight is New Year's Eve, the second New Year's Eve in the past twenty-two years that I have not consumed alcohol, maybe the fourth I have not consumed drugs. I remember one December 31st, in a men's room stall with my girlfriend and her friend, all three of us sucking up cocaine...

Here in rehab, it is not uncommon to see a person kicked out for being in possession of a prosthetic penis connected to a vessel of "clean" urine, which one wears under the clothing in preparation for a random urinalysis. Clean urine...the acquisition and subsequent concealment of, and substitution for "dirty" urine...is as valuable as cigarettes in prison in the movies. In rehab, there is a lot of focus on urine. Much more than in the outside world.

January 1, 2008: Lately in the news there's been a controversy around steroid use by pro athletes. When I was nineteen, I rowed for my college crew team. Of course, we earned no money and received little recognition. Yet I took steroids to be a better competitor. If a guy like me would use steroids to be a third-rate oarsman on an unheralded crew team, it should hardly come as a surprise that a kid around the same age would take them to represent millions of fans, earn a living for his family, compete at the level of his dreams.

January 2, 2008: I used to justify to myself the money I spent on drugs…cocaine, alcohol, ecstasy, etc.… by saying to myself, "Some guys waste all their money on golf; why not spend mine on having a good time with drugs?" I really thought like that.

January 3, 2008: Another couple guys got kicked out of rehab. One received his paycheck, a thousand dollars. He spent the whole thing in one night on crack cocaine and prostitutes. I guess he couldn't handle the responsibility of having a thousand dollars to spend on life's necessities. Or maybe he considered crack and prostitutes to be life's necessities. The next morning, he climbed the fire escape and through the dormitory window. He got kicked out later that day. Another guy got random urine tested and passed clean. He celebrated with a line of coke. He got retested and kicked out the next day.

Yesterday in the news a drunk driver killed a family. Me and some of the other guys sitting around the TV room agreed—it could have just as easily been one of us behind the wheel. We all rolled the same dice, flipped the same cards.

January 5, 2008: The other day in the TV room, a couple guys were talking about how someone they knew mailed psychedelic

Fifteen: Campaigns

mushrooms to a heroin addict, who then flipped to the DEA, and the someone was arrested and transported to the state where he sent the mushrooms. He had to go from one county jail to the next, switching transporting authorities each time. The trip took 28 days, even though he only had to cross a couple state lines. Listening to those guys talk, I began to realize: Concerns like that…the DEA busting me for interstate mushroom transportation…are not things I have to worry about or trouble me anymore. The way such things do not, I would imagine, trouble most people.

January 7, 2008: Today it occurs to me that addiction is my natural predator. I am weak…fearful, resentful, self-seeking… and picked off by addiction the way a lioness lacking swiftness is picked off by wildebeests (or whatever animal is predator to a lioness.) Lack of swiftness is not a trait that benefits lionesses…as fearfulness, resentment, and self-seeking are not traits that benefit me as a human. A swift lioness can outrun the wildebeests that might otherwise prey upon her. A drug addict…like me…is, in theory, able to "outrun" addiction by doing away with fearfulness, resentment, and self-seeking. Nature, it occurs to me, tends to wish to de-select an addict like myself.

January 8, 2008: At the House Meeting, the standard rehab issues get raised…someone has snitched on someone else, the bathrooms are not being cleaned enough by whoever has the clean-the-bathroom chore, items of clothing have disappeared, plates of food wrapped with Saran and clearly labeled have been eaten by someone else. Most of us here in rebab are in our thirties or forties. Maybe a couple guys in their twenties.

Have I ever stolen food? Yes, I have. Have I ever eaten food I found left near a garbage can? Yes, I have done that, too. I have eaten at soup kitchens and homeless shelters and homes I trespassed into. And, of course, I have stolen in order to eat, because my time and what money and energy I had, I devoted to getting high.

January 10, 2008: In Process Group, each of the eight guys speaks for a few minutes on what brought him into rehab, maybe what keeps him here. One guy's father died suddenly last year. Then his fiancée, while pregnant with their first child, took her own life and the life of the unborn baby. She hung herself. He found her.

Tomorrow is my first appointment with a psychiatrist to whom rehab referred me. I still hear disembodied voices and get thoughts about the FBI following me.

January 11, 2008: The psychiatrist diagnoses me with substance-induced psychotic disorder. He mentions medication, but to me it seems taking pills is too much related to what caused the problem that pill-taking would be intended to cure. I compromise with the psychiatrist by going to the nature store for Omega-3 capsules…the psychiatrist told me the effects of drug use are on the blood vessels that supply oxygen to my neurons…he likened my brain to a wedge of Swiss cheese (those are the words he used) and said Omega-3 may help repair the damage.

Today, more than ten years and thousands of pages later, I look back on those blog entries and see I never got much better at writing than those few simple paragraphs, composed at the computer terminal at the Henry Ohlhoff House.

Mark Burnsen reads my blog. Emails his encouragement. His emails are better than my writing. Damn him! He describes driving home from work, past a school where children suffer from various illnesses. Mothers load their kids

Fifteen: Campaigns

in wheelchairs into their cars. Mark thinks about the good fortune life gave him.

Me, I think about who I resent. As I'm writing my blog, I also write a legal brief, a complaint against Stanford University. I file it in federal court.

"YOU ARE TRULY MAKING A FEDERAL CASE OUT OF IT!"

The lawsuit alleges wrongful termination. But the true motivation is to expose the conspiracy...

The FBI, directing me with hypnosis, uses me to expose Stanford...

The FBI tricked me into suing Stanford, which is in fact controlled by organized crime figures who will assassinate me and rid the FBI of me once and for all...

I'm a hypnotically engineered FBI plant, working counterterrorism, and the whole Stanford debacle is a cover story...

From those tangled Bangkok streets, Omar's memory plagues me. To have failed at becoming a Hollywood hero-type, *stopping at nothing* until truth's light shines. Taking the *Sports Illustrated* photo of Poem and I from its protective folder, I scan its borders for subliminal messages. Consumed by fears of the powerful individuals desperate to protect secrets only I can expose.

I do not *imagine it might be true*. I *believe it is.*

I knew Omar.

He worked undercover as Satam al Suqami...things went wrong on board that plane...

Someone else killed Daniel Lewin...

Americans deserve to know the truth...

The truth must be kept secret to protect Americans.

It is all a schizophrenic condition...Omar was just some French guy of Middle Eastern descent...

"HARD TO BELIEVE HUMAN BEINGS WOULD THINK THERE'S ANYTHING SO UNUSUAL ABOUT YOUR BELIEFS," say my constant-companion-disembodied-voices-Boolean-Operator spouse(s).

The FBI is simply stringing me along, waiting to kill me...or worse.

I've talked to the other Americans who were with me in Bangkok and met Omar. None of them seem to believe he could've been other than he claimed. I've found seeming contradictions to the *9/11 Report*...Suqami is reported by the State Department to have been in Riyadh, Saudi Arabia, a couple days before I met Omar in Bangkok. Suqami is supposed to have been in Iran or Bahrain when I knew Omar in Bangkok.

"BUT THESE FACTS STEM FROM THE HIJACKER'S PASSPORT, FOUND ON THE SIDEWALK IN NEW YORK CITY ON SEPTEMBER ELEVENTH!"

Almost everyone else I talk to encourages me to forget the whole thing. Sometimes the encouragement borders on threatening. I'll be considered a *person of interest* if I press too hard.

The Mossad won't hesitate to eliminate me, to prevent the world from learning an Israeli agent was among the hijackers. It's relatively safe for me here in the States, but overseas I could be gotten to. Even today, I'm afraid to leave the country.

A relationship with a woman? Except for a handful of dates, I haven't had one since I got clean. No sex, no kissing, not even a handhold. Too much risk for her—those protecting Omar's secret could use her to get to me. Or is it just the excuse I give myself? Sure, there's other factors...maybe it's okay to hide my schizophrenic condition from family, friends, coworkers, but not from a significant other. I've told enough lies already in pursuit of forms of romance. I've told myself I choose celibacy because of my spirituality—*Don't monks practice abstinence?*—but my relationship with the riddle of Omar supersedes any romantic relationship.

"NOT TO MENTION YOU ARE ALREADY MARRIED!"

Why shouldn't I make these kinds of sacrifices? Plenty of women and men have made far greater. Look no further than our military, our intelligence community.

In February 2008, I could've kept writing my blog about rehab and recovery.

But ultimately, I can't let go of Omar's story.

Schizophrenic episodes compel me to contact journalists. Back when I'd worked at Stanford, I emailed Seymour Hersh at the *New Yorker*. His assistant Lauren sent me a nice response. She wrote Hersh meant to contact me, but I never heard from him (not that I blame him).

Through the years, I'll try many approaches to figuring out who Omar was, why it matters. Including the approach of doing nothing.

For years I believe the FBI monitors my every phone call, email, and text message. Nothing gets through to the recipient unless it's FBI-approved.

It never feels like enough.

It never feels right.

I leave the Ohlhoff House. I stay clean. Giles and Amalia, my friends in the Excelsior, rent me a bedroom in their home. A biotech firm hires me; Alvine Biopharmaceuticals treats me well. Giles and Amalia do too, of course.

None of it is good enough to suit me. I resent it all, and much more. I quit Alvine and move into a North Beach SRO. Figuring I'll find a new job, get my own apartment. But the 2008 economy, like it does for many of us, has other ideas. I get a job cold calling, getting paid commission. I have zero experience in sales; it's the worst economic times since the Great Depression. I'm selling one of the most expensive things there is: flights on private jets.

I obsess over exercise. Go running for an hour, forced to run another hour to get home. Running has endpoints, measures of completion. One can both start and finish a run the same day. I take three hours of yoga classes on the gleaming Bay Club hardwood. Then hit the sauna, steam room, and Jacuzzi. The big-screen TV in the locker room is tuned to ESPN, showing a clip about Lawrence Taylor, the NFL superstar who fell prey to cocaine addiction. Clean towels are stacked by the hundreds on shelves across from the recycling bins.

Outside the Bay Club I unlock my bicycle from a parking meter. A maintenance worker mows the lush grass in the Levi Plaza park. His overalls are covered with grass stains. I pedal up the hill to St. Martin de Porres, a soup kitchen. Underneath a photograph of the Dalai Lama from when he visited there, I gorge myself on the free vegetarian food. Then go to an AA meeting. All the while hearing the disembodied voices of the Boolean Operators as my best friends…

Fifteen: Campaigns

"ARE WE SIMPLY JUST YOUR BEST FRIENDS?"
…my spouse, or spouses…

Such is the life I'm leading when I wander into Joe Alioto's campaign headquarters.

I'd passed the place before. On trips to the public library to borrow yet another addiction memoir. On my way to climb the endless steps of impossibly steep Telegraph Hill, en route to the Bay Club for laps in the heated pool.

"Hey," says the friendly, smiling face of Jeff Dodd, campaign manager, as he shakes my hand. Jeff is a young guy. He could be me just out of college, minus the drugs. "Thanks for stopping by," he says. "You live in the neighborhood?"

"I live…over there," I say, embarrassed, making a vague thumb-jerk in the direction of my SRO. Not a lie, strictly speaking. I'm hoping no bedbugs crawl on me, at least anywhere Jeff can see them. *Sure. I'm just a regular neighborhood guy.*

"So, what can we do for you?" Jeff keeps smiling.

"I was wondering…are you looking for volunteers? I've volunteered before…for the Red Cross. Um, at a homeless shelter." The Red Cross gig was one of the most fulfilling jobs I'd done. Working in the disaster center after Hurricane Katrina, assisting those forced to relocate to the Bay Area.

"What is it you like about Joe Alioto?" Jeff asks. I mutter something about admiring Joe's work on the Police Commission. Like I'd read about on the internet. Turns out I have Joe mixed up with one of his relatives. But if Jeff Dodd picks up on my mistake, he doesn't let on. "Excellent!!" he says. "Leave your number; we'll call you tomorrow and let you know."

The next twenty-four hours present additional concerns—on top of the average fears of FBI conspiracies to send me to prison, and the tide of American sentiment having turned against me for failing to expose the truth about the 9/11 coverup…and whether I remembered to drop off my dry cleaning.

What if Joe Alioto's campaign won't have me? If they find out about my drug history, my misdemeanor convictions?

"WHAT IF THEY DISCRIMINATE AGAINST THE DISEMBODIED?"

Turns out neither I nor the Boolean Operators have cause to worry. Jeff Dodd calls the next day. I go to work on the campaign. Making phone calls, attending rallies, helping out in miscellaneous ways.

I find a home amongst the other volunteers. We have one volunteer, Mr. Magic. A San Francisco North Beach original. Mr. Magic is working for Joe's campaign while he's also running for President of the United States. We have Horace, a former professional boxer who, like me, is recently clean off meth. Horace shows up at HQ early in the morning, stuffs a handful of window-signs in his satchel, and gets a list of addresses from Jeff Dodd. Hops on his ten-speed and rides around the precincts ringing doorbells, delivering those window signs to supporters.

Soon enough I meet Joe Alioto. He takes a couple of us volunteers walking the precincts. Ringing doorbells, greeting voters. I hold a campaign sign. Some voters won't come to the door. They pull back curtains and raise Venetian blinds to stare down from their windows. Joe doesn't mind. He smiles up from the sidewalk. "Hi! I'm Joe Alioto. I'd like to be your supervisor."

Fifteen: Campaigns

They smile back. It's okay…it's just Joe Alioto, neighborhood guy. And the guy next to him, holding the campaign sign? He must be okay, too.

Joe wants to meet every citizen he'd represent as supervisor ("supervisor" is like San Francisco's version of city council member.) You meet him and see a handsome, young guy. If you've lived in San Francisco for a while, maybe you recognize his name. Joe's grandfather was mayor—credited for making possible the Transamerica Pyramid. Joe's got family connections, education, solid career opportunities. His wife Erica is a senior manager at a big firm. They're expecting their first child in the next couple months. Joe's got plenty of whatever most of us might want to feel successful. Yet he runs for office—pursuing public service, forsaking an easy life—because he wants to make the North Beach neighborhood where he grew up a better place.

The Cellar Hole may be a continent and a psychological world away, but I learn to want to be the kind of man Joe is. To use what life gave me to do good for others.

Later, Joe and I eat sandwiches at a sidewalk table on Columbus Avenue. "So, Ed," he says, friendly, curious, "what's your story?"

It's tempting to set aside the story of the meth.

Hide the past, bury the shame.

Look who I'm sitting across the table from! I want the grandson of the man who helped make the Transamerica Pyramid possible to like me. To feel I'm worthy of friendship. Yet something inside me knows…if I'm going to be a writer, I'm going to have to learn to speak a certain truth.

I decide to start a campaign of my own.

"Well, Joe…I grew up," I say, "in this small town, back in Massachusetts. I came out here when I was sixteen." Already I've figured out, when talking about being an addict, skip the endless preamble. It's natural to want to pile on details, rationales, explanations. But listeners tune out. The audience appreciates the succinct. You can paint enough of a picture in sixty seconds. I give Joe the rundown: college, biotech career, owning a home…

I take a deep breath…

"But, Joe, you know…all along, I was a drug addict."

Joe listens to my story. Jail, destitution, psychosis. I don't tell him I still hear voices—I'm a decade away from being forthcoming about my schizophrenia-like condition. But I tell Joe most of the details.

He doesn't ask me to leave the campaign.

Not by a long shot.

He asks me to accompany him working the bus stops. Meeting voters as they wait for the lumbering MUNI coaches on their morning commutes to work. Joe shakes hands, puts forth his ideas. Sure, he's a good salesman. But his ideas bring good value. At first, I simply stand back and hold a campaign sign. Yet soon I've absorbed enough of Joe's platform; can speak to it myself.

I start shaking hands with voters, too.

The campaign brings me on board as a paid staffer. Soon I have the key to HQ, open and close the place. Train new volunteers. Less than a year ago, I was conducting experiments in glass ashtrays in my room at the SRO. Nowhere near someone you'd trust with a key, or a paycheck, or to be in charge of

Fifteen: Campaigns

anything. I meet Gavin Newsom. Then mayor of San Francisco, now governor of California. Up close he comes across like a hard-nosed politician from the old days. Like you might meet in the pages of *The Glass Key* or some other Dashiell Hammett novel. Not a soft case at all.

One morning after commute hour, Joe and I take a coffee break. "So, Ed," he says, "how's it going with you?" We share a table at Mario's Bohemian Cigar Store Cafe. Across Union Street, in Washington Square and beneath the twin spires of Saints Peter and Paul church, dozens of Asian-Americans practice tai chi. They move in unison—arms, legs, and torsos like waves sweeping onto a beach.

"I'm good, Joe. One year today, clean off meth."

"That's great, Ed!" Joe's smile is a million watts. As bright as Uncle Jupiter's.

"A year ago, I was in bad shape."

"Well, you've worked hard, got back on track." *Back on track.* The same words Officer Pagano used when she arrested me four years ago. Joe drains the last of his espresso. "So, Ed…election day is two weeks away. Hopefully we'll win. But this other guy, David Chiu, he's doing pretty well. Anyway, you should have a plan for what happens if we don't." He looks out the plateglass window at the tai chi practitioners in Washington Square.

"How's your writing coming along?" he says after a while.

"It's coming," I say. "I wrote a short story."

"Awesome! You should submit it."

"I don't know…"

"Ed. Submit it. You're a great writer. Have you ever thought of going to a writer's workshop? Like the one they have in Idaho."

I consider this. "No...I just never thought something like that...could be for me."

"Well, look. If you want to go...and I don't know what's involved...Erica and I, we can help sponsor you."

I never end up going to the Idaho Writers Conference. I wish I had! But I don't have the confidence yet.

In the years to come, Joe and Erica invite me to family Easter and Christmas gatherings...

They give me countless references for interviews and leads on jobs in the challenging days of '08—'09.

The reason I become friends with Joe, that he and Erica encouraged my writing? I told Joe about my meth addiction. Sure, if I hadn't, I'm sure he would've liked me anyway. But I wouldn't have become close to him and Erica.

Sometimes what seems like our greatest weaknesses are our greatest strengths.

One thing we drug addicts have in common: obstacles.

We put them in front of ourselves; others put them there.

It doesn't always matter where they came from...when we quit drugs, we've overcome an obstacle. *Others admire that.* Often times, anyway; sure, you'll encounter those who fixate on others' past mistakes and current shortcomings. Who knows why? Maybe they haven't fully come to terms with their own pasts and presents. I've done this myself, plenty of times, and often catch myself at it today. Yet a lot of people hear a story of overcoming drug addiction and think, *I can make positive changes in my life, too.* Even if that person is Joe Alioto, soon to be first-time father, closing in on becoming an elected official (we're leading in the polls at one point). For me to

Fifteen: Campaigns

understand—someone like Joe can learn something from me? It's a powerful feeling.

We don't win the campaign for San Francisco Supervisor (David Chiu, the winner, is currently serving in the California State Assembly.) A letdown, to be sure. I'd envisioned myself working for Joe in City Hall. Getting deeply involved in the North Beach community I would've been helping him represent. Fantasies of Joe following in his grandfather's footsteps to become mayor. Me with a career in city government. Writing a book about the experience.

Thanks to Joe and Erica, other dreams are possible. When they kept their minds open to the possibility that a man less than a year gone from being "Reggie" could find his way to being a part of society, my mind opened too. Quitting drugs may have won me a battle, but until others helped me discover how to live a meaningful life without drugs, I was a long way from winning the war.

Joe and Erica allow me to see how that meaningful life is possible. They show me how to *project positivity*. To find ways to treat others with admiration and respect. Even if I don't *feel it*. Especially then.

The 12 steps have a saying: It's easier to act our way into right thinking than to think our way into right acting. I crusade against my own negativity and resentments by treating others well (striving to, anyway, and striving harder when I fall short, which is often). I find ways to focus on what's going right. That which we focus on expands. I spent enough of my life complaining, lying, being negative. You saw where it got me.

Thus, the path is set.

Yet many obstacles remain along the way.

Fortunately, along with those obstacles will come the help to move past them.

On the campaign trail with Joe Alioto (photo: Max Cohen)

Sixteen:
Tigers' Cave

There are only two ways to live your life.
One is as though nothing is a miracle.
The other is as though everything is a miracle.

—Albert Einstein

I give a name to my suicidal depression.

(I like giving things funny little names.)

I call it the Spalding Grey Portcullis.

Spalding Grey was an accomplished writer and actor, really terrific.

He had a terrible car wreck in Ireland…

It's not clear (from my research) the extent to which his injuries led to his taking his life.

(He took his life in 2004, a year before Hunter S. Thompson took his.)

A portcullis—this much is clear—is a massive door sealing the gateway to a castle. If marauders lay siege, the portcullis keeps them out. People inside are kept safe.

Or you could say they're trapped.

When the Spalding Grey Portcullis clangs down, I'm entombed within a stone tower. My thoughts are peasants dressed in rags. My thoughts want to walk with the long-gone Mickey, long to return to the home on Monterey Boulevard.

I had it all…how could I have thrown it all away?

My SRO is filled with bedbugs. I wake to feel them crawl across my face. In the hallway outside my door, human feces had appeared. I'd almost stepped in them, going to the common bathroom in the middle of the night.

When the Spalding Gray Portcullis shuts, I resign myself to a lifetime spent behind it. A hallmark of depression.

A broken bone? We know…*it will mend.*

Catch the flu? *It won't last forever.*

Depression is for life. It's sure the way it seems, anyway.

The Golden Gate Bridge is maybe an hour's walk. Someone once told me most jumpers leap from the side facing the city. The Transamerica Pyramid's dagger plunging up at Heaven. *Goodbye cruel world.* It seems reasonable! Write a goodbye mass e-mail. Hit the send button. Step over the feces in the hallway. Arrive at the foot of the Bridge. Maybe turn to look for the Burger King, where Victor and I ate hamburgers before another night at the Royal Gate vodka and beer. Real cinematic stuff. Then begin the long climb to the bottom of the sea.

"YOU SEEM MILDLY TROUBLED. PERHAPS YOU MIGHT DO WITH A NICE HYPNOTIST?"

A what?

"A HYPNOTIST!"

Indeed…

I often suspect the Booleans are a product of hypnotic suggestions beamed through HyperSonic Sound. Maybe the Mossad is behind it all. Perhaps a hypnotist can break it?

Sixteen: Tigers' Cave

"ONE MUST CONSIDER ALL THE ANGLES."

After a quick internet search and a couple phone calls, we're on my way to my first hypnosis session. I have high hopes, believe me.

"ONE MUST HAVE HIGH HOPES!"

Marty Diamond is my hypnotist. A long time ago, doctors told him he had cancer. They sentenced him to Not So Long to Live. What does Marty do? Buys a fifty-pound bag of rice and makes his way to a hut in the Canadian wilderness. Old Marty had decided he was gonna figure out how to heal himself with meditation. His first night out, he almost got eaten by a bear. But Marty, he taught himself self-hypnosis. He made his cancer disappear.

He hypnotizes me a few times. It seems to work pretty well. I stop eating so much food for a while. "But," Marty says, "you should really be meditating, too." Sounds okay to me.

"WHAT HAVE YOU GOT TO LOSE?"

Marty invites me to join the Tigers' Cave meditation group. We meet in his apartment. The first night, I take the bus. I'm apprehensive. Sitting with serious meditators...*can I do this?* It feels like Thanksgiving in Bangkok, on the eve of Muay Thai camp. But at the same time, it's like joining a secret club. Like hanging out with the drinkers and drug-takers, in a weird way.

On Marty's bookshelves, dozens of manuals on martial arts coexist with volumes on spirituality. A life-sized self-defense striking dummy, the Body Opponent Bag (BOB), looking like a bare-chested storefront mannequin, gazes impassively over the head of a small statue of Buddha. Marty tells me, "Come on in; sit down." Points towards a meditation cushion. I have to step over a pair of boxing gloves.

Marty rings a small bell to begin our sitting. He meditates four hours a day, sitting in full lotus. He doesn't use a cushion. He spent something like seven years in the Rochester Zen Center. Can you imagine that? Seven years. He was an actor, too. Was in a movie with Jeff Goldblum. He was a writer—interviewed Mike Tyson back before Tyson was champion. Marty published an article in *Sports Illustrated*.

Donnelly sits to my left, wearing an Adidas track suit. He meditates in half-lotus—hurt his knee playing soccer. These days he's more of a coach than a player. His youth teams make it to state championships. Some soccer coaches in England get wind of how well his kids do and fly Donnelly out to consult for them.

So, the three of us are sitting as silent BOB stares off into the distance. "Imagine something," Marty says. Already I like where this is going. Marty uses these metaphors. Metaphors are good when you want to get a grip on things. "Imagine you're outside at night. There's a full moon." I can picture the full moon up above my Cellar Hole. Even though I never played out there at night.

"The moonlight," Marty says, "illuminates your surroundings. In a sense, it does. See, the moon is really a rock in the sky. It has no light of its own...*it reflects the sun's light*. We're like the moon. We appear to give off our own light. In a sense we do... but we are really reflecting the light of the Spirit."

I think about that for a while. There's some force, some *spirit*, and I reflect her light. I'll spend the next decade pondering old

Sixteen: Tigers' Cave

Marty Diamond's lessons. I'm glad he never got eaten by that bear up in Canada. I'm happy he proved his doctors wrong.

We meditate for thirty minutes. My mind plays a trick or two.

"YOU KNOW HOW YOUR MIND GETS!"

My mind pictures Donnelly, Marty, and myself, like we're these three massive stone statues. About a mile high. We're surrounding a castle courtyard. The castle's inhabitants, the peasants and knights and maybe even the king and queen, rush about. They run around and ride horses in the courtyard, which is really the shag in Marty Diamond's carpet. They perceive us three meditators yet are unable to understand our nature.

The bell chimes. Marty brews a pot of green tea. I open the bag of organic chocolate chip cookies I've brought. There's a Whole Foods store about a block away from Marty's. Donnelly doesn't want a cookie…he's not eating sugar. He takes tea and rubs his injured knee.

"I've worked with clients who are suicidal," Marty says. We're sitting and drinking tea. "I tell them, if you commit suicide, you get sent backwards through multiple previous lifetimes."

This kind of stuff seems to happen all the time. Synchronicities, and the like. I haven't mentioned my suicidal thoughts to Marty, never talked about the Spalding Gray Portcullis. But Marty, it's like he has some kind of weird power, knowing to say stuff like this. Marty instills a belief in me—to kill myself would mean going backwards through many lifetimes. This is really the only reason I don't kill myself. Hey, I don't even want to repeat *this lifetime*, much less go backwards through others. Marty gets me believing this life is just one stage along a vast journey.

It starts to make sense…

I'm after these goals—I've *been after* these goals—career, fitness, etcetera. There's nothing wrong with these goals. But they aren't of *lasting value*.

What *is* worth pursuing in this lifetime? *That's* what I want to know. All I know is, if I'm looking to be certain about the future, one thing in particular springs to mind…death. Not to get maudlin or anything, but our friend the grim reaper will show up one day. Why not kill myself? Life behind the Spalding Gray Portcullis…when it seems certain *it will never feel any different*…seems hardly worth living. But Marty gets me thinking about doing what God—whoever or whatever God is, if God even exists—put me here to do.

I begin a meditation practice. I sit almost every morning. Rising early, often before dawn. The Boolean Operators do this weird, annoying thing. If I recite a mantra to myself, in my head, the Boolean Operators repeat it. I can hear them outside my window. It's the one time they're hard to tune out. It gets frustrating…who wants to hear disembodied voices when you're trying to *meditate*, of all things? Eventually it dawns on me: Meditators travel thousands of miles to meditate among chanting monks, right? They spend their life savings, maybe. With the Boolean Operators? I have my own version of monks chanting, without even needing to leave my SRO hotel room. Without so much as disturbing my friends the bedbugs.

Sometimes I meditate thirty minutes and all I can think about is what shirt to wear. Often resentments and negativity creep in. Sexual fantasies. Heroic daydreams. I'll compose emails in my mind. *Controlling the mind is like trying to control the wind,* as it says in the Bhagavad-Gita.

Sixteen: Tigers' Cave

"IT SEEMS TRUE ENOUGH."

Meditation helps manage the rage. The rage boils like a screaming teakettle with the flame turned past high. The rage is directed at strangers, passing motorists, someone waiting on the BART train platform. I get gripped by visions of homicidal violence. Envisioning myself pulling drivers out of their vehicles, smashing heads into rear-view mirrors. Fantasies of screaming matches, heaving furniture across rooms. Kicking down doors that close off my exits. The scenes replay again and again. I try and make them stop, but it's like trying to make a toothache go away just by thinking about it.

I read a lot of books by addicts who got sober. There was this one called *Dreamseller* by Brandon Novak. He writes for a former drug addict, rage is like a mini-high. When I imagine the homicidal violence, there's a burst of adrenalin. It seems to trigger some biochemical process my brain has grown to depend upon. Then I get guilty. Like I'm indulging myself with the rage. But it's like a car alarm going off somewhere nearby. Incessant, needless blares, disturbing all within a multi-block radius, probably because a bus rolled past. You wait and wait, knowing the car alarm blasts have to stop *sometime*. But while the horn keeps shocking the senses, it makes it hard to think of anything else. But meditation helps me control my actions. Rarely do I employ even strong language.

It's far from easy to force myself along the path of spirituality and meditation. Never a flash of blinding light; never an *unwavering belief* my path is right. Uncertainty is one of the few constants. Doubt, fear, and anger are as much a part of my spiritual practice as faith, compassion, and love. The times I'm most sure of myself are usually the times I'm most struggling. Fortunately, others will lift my spirits for me.

Donnelly rides into my life like an armored saint in an Adidas tracksuit. Tigers' Cave session ends, and he's got about fifty other places to be, but he never minds giving me a ride home. He pulls into the bus stop outside my North Beach SRO and lets his black Mercedes' engine idle. Donnelly spent his youth the way I wish I'd had the courage to spend mine. In some ways, anyhow—on the athletic fields, for instance. As a leader in his peer group. Although that's not the way Donnelly or his long-ago rivals might phrase it.

Donnelly was a leader of a San Francisco neighborhood association known as Sunset District Incorporated. As you might guess, the guys from the Sunset District didn't "incorporate" in order to satisfy certain IRS requirements. They weren't like what you think of today's gangs. SDI guys drank and fought with their fists. They showed up to USF parties like Delta Force in Blackhawks. Well-organized, with a plan for how the party would end. It wasn't the same plan drunken college kids like me had in mind.

I don't mean to glamorize fighting and drunken college parties. Believe me, I *wish* I'd skipped all those parties, and studied in the library instead. But you can only stop life on the dime you're on today. Today, Donnelly owns businesses, leads his community, and helps others looking to leave their old lives behind. Like Erica and Joe Alioto, Donnelly has a lot of people to choose from when it comes to hanging out. He chooses to hang out with me.

Sixteen: Tigers' Cave

We sit in his Mercedes in front of my SRO. Up the hill, neon cappuccino steam floats behind plate-glass cafe windows. To draw in tourists, like the couple from Montana to whom I tried to sell my haikus right after poor old Hunter S. Thompson shotgunned himself. Donnelly nods sagely while I talk of UFO sightings and moon landing theories. Who else can you talk to about stuff like this? Donnelly is a legend of the Sunset District, then and now. Someone I can feel safe around. In life, you don't exactly encounter whole armies of people who make you feel safe.

"Donnelly," I say, "there's a story…I haven't told it much. When I was a college freshman, I had a friend, Janet. She went to Cambridge Rindge and Latin High School, in Boston. She used to tutor Patrick Ewing. One night, she brings me to her uncle's house for dinner. I don't remember much…we borrowed Phyllis' car; Logan came along." I fill Donnelly in on who Phyllis and Logan were. "Anyway…years later, Janet calls me at my parents' home. She says, 'Did you hear about my uncle?' It turns out, her uncle's real name was Jimmy Smyth. He escaped from the Maze Prison in 1983; was living underground here in San Francisco until he turned himself in.

"I want to be a writer," I say. "Maybe I'll write about Jimmy Smyth."

"Here's a story you can use," Donnelly says, shutting off the engine. Young women and men are passing along on the sidewalk. Maybe headed from yoga class, or to the bars for a drink. Or home to bed to rise for work early tomorrow. People can be on their way to or from almost anywhere.

"I was in Northern Belfast," Donnelly says, "in a bar, with

another guy named Jimmy. Jimmy the Seaman." Donnelly's got his hands in sort of a prayer position. But he's not praying, of course. His wrists are over the steering wheel. His fingers point forward, like the prow of a ship. "Jimmy, he told me he wanted to show me something. So, I followed him out back, to an alley. Now, I was scared…Belfast is a spooky place, you know? And there's a war going on…. We're out there in the alley, and Jimmy, he reaches into his jacket pocket. I'm thinking he's gonna come out with a gun, right? Like he thinks I'm a spy."

"Or it could be a test," I say. I'm getting all riled up. You know you're getting all riled up when you point out something obvious like it's some big revelation. "Like he wanted to see if you were nervous, and why would you have reason to be?"

"Right." Donnelly zips the front of his sweatsuit jacket up under his chin. "I stand stock-still," he says. "I don't want to look afraid, you know? But Jimmy, all he pulls out is a photograph. He asks me if I know the guys…they're wearing bellbottoms, long hair. That was the look back then, like Bobby Sands. Jimmy, he tells me the men in the picture were murdered. For being touts."

I imagine the photograph Donnelly saw in a Belfast alley. Young men, looking perhaps like Logan and I, freshman year of college. "Touts," I say, "that's like a spy?"

Donnelly nods, shifts so his knee is more comfortable. "Jimmy asks me if I believe it. I say, 'I don't know, Jimmy.' And Jimmy, he says they were three of the best fighters they had." By "they," I know who Donnelly means. And somehow I know what's coming next. "He tells me these were his sons," Donnelly says. "That the order to have them murdered came from the top. That's how Jimmy knew the war was rigged. That the British were constructing buildings and blowing them up themselves. They had infiltrators at the highest levels."

Up the hill from us, the neon sign outside the Italian restaurant goes out. They're all closed up for the night. Lights behind windows in the apartment building blink off, too. Apartment-dwellers going to sleep. Just up the hill there's the cafe where I get my morning coffee…a speck of dim light behind the plate-glass window. There are so many little things to notice.

"Anyway, not long after I met Jimmy the Seaman, there's this little article in the newspaper about Freddie Scappaticci. They called him Stakeknife. Just a tiny article, you know? You could easily overlook it."

Later, up in my hotel room, I switch on my laptop and read how Freddie Scappaticci was in the IRA's Internal Security Unit. The ISU investigated leaks and exposed touts.

"WE ARE EXPLORING OUR CONNECTIONS TO THE IRISH REPUBLICAN ARMY!"

Maybe…but more like, in Donnelly I've found another person who *I want to be like*. Fortunately for me, I get to spend a lot of time with Donnelly in the years to come. We train in the gym, go for walks by the beach and around Lake Merritt. He invites me to his family gatherings. Rarely will he fail to impart some form of spiritual wisdom. Donnelly has studied near-death experiences, studied the Bible. He embodies a form of spirituality different from any I knew existed. Donnelly can talk about his personal experience learning the IRA was infiltrated, and be comfortable with who he is, *and* remain a spiritual person highly respected in his communities.

If Donnelly is an armored Saint, Bryan is an angel investor. His investment is in me as a human being; as person worth bringing back to life. I'm at the Bay Club one morning, making my way through the basketball gym. Headed upstairs to the AstroTurf tennis courts to hit from the ball machine and listen to the Boolean Operators.

"LIKE A YOUNG BORIS BECKER MIGHT HAVE DONE!"

Bryan is alone on the hardwood. Shooting 3-pointers; wearing ear buds. He was a couple years ahead of me in college. But we had some of the same friends; knew each other in passing. "How's it going?" Bryan's smiling, seems genuinely glad to see me. He takes his ear buds out, dribbles his basketball a few times. After a little small talk, who from college is doing what and such, I start in. "You know…I had some problems." I fumble around with the drug story.

"Well, you look good now." He smiles and tosses me the basketball. "Want to play some one-on-one?"

I set down my tennis racquet and dribble the basketball off my foot. I have to chase it halfway to the swimming pool. I heave it back towards Bryan, but my aim is no good and it flies wild. Now he has to run it down. But we get into a game. Soon, we're playing hoops every morning.

We play one-on-one, running full court the width of the floor. Bryan usually wins. He is a serious athlete. Used to be a hard-core triathlete and broke records on the ergometers (the type of rowing machines Olympic oarsmen train on). I try and keep up with him; my skills improve somewhat. I hustle on defense, teach myself a weird kind of hook shot.

Sixteen: Tigers' Cave

On breaks between games we talk no-carb diets, target heart rates, training zones.

Bryan's got a major career in the financial industry. He sits on the board of a nonprofit delivering after-school programs to tens of thousands of kids, mostly youth of color. He's just met his girlfriend, Melissa. She's another source of inspiration for me to keep doing better. She graduated a top college, excels in her career. Her workout routine makes Bryan and my basketball games look like a couple guys playing underhand catch with a corduroy beanbag. And Melissa is another someone who *cares about me*, the way I am.

Bryan and Melissa find an apartment together. He asks if I can help him move; picks me up outside the Bay Club. When we arrive at the new place, he wants me to carry a framed picture and a couple of shirts—on hangers, in their dry-cleaning clear plastic—up a flight of stairs.

That's all.

I realize…Bryan doesn't *need* help moving. He *wants* me to feel like I'm contributing. Like I'm part of his and Melissa's life. Bryan puts me in touch with a couple of those college friends I pushed away. With my friend who asked me to be his best man, whose wedding I didn't show up to. And with two of those friends who were at my intervention; at the UCSF emergency room.

There are a lot of mornings I wake up in my SRO, not finding much reason to get out of bed. But then I remember. Bryan's gonna be waiting for me on the Bay Club hardwood. He's invested in my recovery…I can't let him down.

I'm grateful for Bryan, his patience, his faith in me. He sees something in me I don't see in myself. Were I to guess at what Bryan gets for himself out of our friendship? The chance to make a big difference in the life of one person (me), yes. But Bryan, he's an investor, and investors get returns. He believes—he *knows*—his investment in me will make a difference in others' lives, too.

Someone once told me any person is the average of the few individuals closest to him or her. If that's true? I'm in luck, my first few years clean off meth. Those are very hard years… with the Spalding Gray Portcullis, the obsessions over Omar, the food issues. But Joe and Erica Alioto taught me to respect others, to be polite, appreciative…to show those around me the positive sides of my feelings. Marty Diamond showed me the path to a meditation practice and gave me reason not to kill myself. Donnelly gives me a way, now that I've chosen to exist in this world, to feel like I can be part of it. Bryan and Melissa teach me I'm not gonna let myself be the person who lets down my investors.

Thanks to these people in my life, I can keep moving forward.

I'm helping Sebastian move his friend Julie out of her apartment. I've never met Julie. I'm never gonna meet her. She relapsed. Called Sebastian from the roof of her apartment building. Drunk, set to leap.

"I called her dad," Sebastian says. Unlike Bryan, he's putting me to *work*. We're hoisting a couch through a doorway. It weighs about twelve tons. "I didn't know what else to do." He grunts, gets his end through the doorway, sets it down. I'm pushed up between the couch and the wall, barely able to breathe. Sebastian comes around to help me. "Damn," he says, once we've got the thing out into the hall. "Let's take a break." It sounds good to me.

"So, what happened to her?" I follow him into Julie's kitchen.

"Julie? Her dad flew up and brought her to rehab." He takes some bread from a cabinet, opens the fridge. "You want a turkey sandwich?"

"Maybe just the turkey. I'm doing a no-carb diet."

"Oh, yeah? How does that work?"

"I'm losing weight." I don't tell him about the food obsessions. If you've ever been obsessed with food, maybe you know how it is. *If I can control my food, I can control my life.* Subconsciously, losing weight equates to making myself disappear. "I'm doing sun-gazing, too." I drop a piece of turkey on the floor, brush it off, eat it. "You stare at the sun for a few seconds every day."

"Sounds like you're gonna go blind."

"There's times when it's safe. Right after the sun rises and before it sets. Supposedly you sun-gaze and you don't have to eat."

Sebastian takes a bite of sandwich and leans against the kitchen counter. "Julie was doing good." He chews, drums his fingers. He sits at a table big enough for two. Maybe where Julie sat, when she drank her last drink before going up on the roof. "This must've been hers." He taps the cover of an AA big book near wilting flowers in a blue glass bottle. "When she called me," he glances at the sky, "she said…" He blinks a few times, rubs his forehead. "She said she wasn't honest. You know, they say we're only as sick as our secrets." He pushes away his plate with his unfinished sandwich.

"So how you really doing, Ed?"

I shrug, eat the last of my turkey. "Everything's good," I say.

I fast for five days straight. The Boolean Operators congratulate me. "MAKE SURE TO BREAK THE FAST WITH SOMETHING SMALL. LIKE A TOMATO!"

We become vegan, the Boolean Operators and I. On Sunday nights, Uncle Jupiter goes out of his way to ensure the dinner menu has vegan options when he takes us to the country club. He brings me to baseball games and a basketball game at U.C. Berkeley. Drives me to the airport for 6:00 a.m. flights to go back and visit my parents. "When you see them," he says, patting my leg, double-parked outside the airport, "focus on what's right. Don't worry about what's wrong."

Truer words never spoken, Uncle Jupe.

My family is like a distant mountain range. Seen from the deck of a ship, bobbing in an ocean far from shore. I'm still convinced Uncle Jupiter and my parents know *something* about why the FBI is after me. I'm convinced they were in on the conspiracies from the beginning. You don't just shrug these things off. You don't quite know how to handle them, either.

My family expects me to work in biotech; take home a dependable paycheck. And why not? They survived that way. They can't be expected to understand their solutions to life's problems won't work for me. It's not so much there's something wrong with my family…you can find something wrong with almost every family, if you look hard enough.

I'm wrong for my family.

Sixteen: Tigers' Cave

At least that's how it feels, when that old Spalding Gray Portcullis shuts me in.

The struggles continue for years.

It gets better.

During the times behind the Portcullis I focus on the spirituality taught by Marty Diamond, Donnelly, and program-goers in the 12-step meetings. Strive to come to a deeper understanding of the Universal Force, the Great Spirit...always trying to keep straight what I *know* versus what I *believe*. Reading and re-reading the Bhagavad Gita, having conversations with Buddhists, Rabbis...

"WE HAVE ATTENDED RABBINICAL COLLEGE!"

Real rabbis and other spiritual leaders...not their Boolean versions. I attend countless 12-step meetings. At 6:00 a.m. I can often be found occupying a seat at the Dry Dock, the AA clubhouse in the Marina District. My copy of the Big Book looks like the Northern Lights, with all the highlighting. I think constantly about the Higher Power...to paraphrase something from George Harrison: *Everything can wait, except the search for spiritual meaning.* Harrison was in the Beatles, considered by many one of the greatest rock n' roll bands in history. Yet Harrison is saying, even the very heights of rock n' roll stardom can wait. The search for spiritual meaning cannot.

I've been writing. Soon after I met him, Marty Diamond read one of my short stories. Like Joe Alioto, he encouraged me to publish it. He suggested *SoMa Lit,* an online literary magazine published by Scott James, who later had a regular column in the *New York Times* (to my knowledge, Scott never contributed to any research on HyperSonic Sound). *SoMa*

Lit publishes my story. It's a strange piece. One of the lead characters has the same name as me. He's the doorman at a strip club, just like I stood in my tuxedo outside the Hustler Club during my last, catastrophic year on meth. As the story progresses, he has fantasies about stabbing a customer to death in insane rage.

When Scott publishes my work, there's a feeling of triumph.

"WE ARE OVERJOYED WITH ELATION!"

A newspaper called the *City Star* publishes my article about the withholding of federal grant money for mental health services. I envision sweeping success; start swinging for the fences. Over the course of the next ten years, I write screenplays, novels, short stories. Certain my name will leap from the pages of the *City Star* to a theater marquee or bookstore window display. I churn out pages. Rise hours before my temp job at the University of California, in order to write. Bring my laptop to work, write on the shuttle rides and lunch breaks.

It always seems to end in frustration. Literary agents turn down my submissions. I just miss Robin Williams backstage at a comedy show (he would've agreed on the spot to star in the screenplay I wrote for him, of course). The self-doubt can derail you, surer than anything on the outside. Almost all of my writing goes unseen, except for by the eyes of a small few. They encourage me, but…

They're just being nice, I tell myself.

"THUS, DOES THE WORLD OF LITERATURE CONTINUE TO SUFFER FROM YOUR LACK OF CONTRIBUTIONS."

The Boolean Operators may be joking.

Sixteen: Tigers' Cave

The Spalding Gray Portcullis is serious.

Thanks to Marty Diamond, I won't kill myself. Yet I wish I could. Life is an ocean of mired-ness. Mired in depression. Islands here and there. Going to the movies, for instance. That's an island. I go to movies by myself. I stop at Trader Joe's for a bag of organic popcorn with olive oil and smuggle it into the independent films at the Embarcadero Theater. There's the island of having dinner with Uncle Jupiter and Aunt Koral (filtering out Jupiter's pointed questions as to what I'm doing with my life—that's just him being him). Reading books puts me on an island. There are all these books by undercover cops: *No Angel: My Harrowing Undercover Journey to the Inner Circle of the Hells Angels*, by Jay Dobyns; *Collura: Actor with a Gun*, by Bill Davidson; *Donnie Brasco*. I read addiction memoirs: *Broken: My Story of Addiction and Redemption*, by William Cope Moyers. I get to meet Moyers at a dinner one night. He's a nice guy, very encouraging. He wrote a great memoir. There's about a million addiction memoirs out there.

Outside of those islands, the mired-ness. The drudged-through-muck feeling *this is life, and there's nothing more*. Slogging through another workout. Obsessed with exercise, whether enough calories got burned. Terrified tomorrow I'll lose control and eat a chocolate donut…one will turn into a dozen will turn into another run at the meth pipe. Any loss of control has the potential to spiral into a return to drugs. And we know where that will end. Discipline—especially when it comes to exercise and diet—has become an obsession in and of itself.

My lower teeth are flecked with a crusted black moss, impossible to scrape away. My digestive system seems overrun with…

something…as evidenced by excessive escaping flatulence, belching stomach gas. A strange cyst develops on the top of my head, like a miniature horn. Eventually I'll find dentists, doctors…homeopaths, an acupuncturist. But in those early days of being clean, I feel—at some level—my physical conditions serve to keep others away. And the further away others are, the closer my thoughts remain.

Omar intrudes into my thoughts.

It's the public's right to know an infiltrator was among the hijackers.

It's in the best interests of counterterrorism the public does not know the truth about Satam al Suqami…yet.

It's not a matter of *whether* the FBI is involved in my life; it's a matter of *how*. It's not like I'm *choosing* to think about Omar. I *have to*. Someone told me once, if there's something you *want to do*, then you can do it or not. In the big picture, the eternal view, maybe it doesn't even make all that much difference.

But if there's something you *have to do?* You may be afraid—or confused. You may feel yourself a failure, as I did for much of the time I considered the story of Omar. Plenty of people—everyone, probably—believe themselves failures at times. F. Scott Fitzgerald drank himself to death when he couldn't make it as a Hollywood screenwriter. Even if you're not a big reader, you've heard of *The Great Gatsby*.

Omar runs ahead of me, on the wide Bangkok boulevard, as speeding chunks of steel and churning fuel speed past…

Thoughts of the Golden Gate Bridge, that last look at the Transamerica Pyramid on the way down.

The Spalding Gray Portcullis, solid in place.

Yet in 2013, something arrives to begin to break down the Portcullis' iron bars.

I discover Krav Maga.

Seventeen:

Krav Maga

The counterattack is not a defensive action but a method of using the opponent's offense as a means of the successful completion of one's own attack. The counterattack is an advanced phase of offense...it is the greatest art of fighting, the art of the champion.

—Bruce Lee

I'd passed the Krav Maga Institute on my way to a Tigers' Cave. Peeked in the window. Saw the punching bags, swinging like those in the Bangkok Muay Thai Academy. Standing a watch like the Body Opponent Bag in Marty Diamond's living room.

I didn't know Krav is an Israeli system of self-defense. Heavy on situational awareness, fitness, and brutal counterassaults...

But somehow, something inside me knew I had to find my way into that Krav Maga studio.

Fitness is a main way to stay distracted behind the Spalding Gray Portcullis. Countless hours of lifting weights, running, yoga. Anything to keep the endorphins flowing, channel the obsessions away from getting wasted. Something's gotta occupy the mind, right?

Seventeen: Krav Maga

"YES!" The Boolean Operators agree. "THE MIND MUST REMAIN UNENCUMBERED."

I force myself into the discipline of *never missing a workout*. Rising at 3:00 a.m., dragging the Booleans along, fighting off the flu, skipping a social event? No matter what, I get in my exercise. With the Spalding Gray Portcullis as the main alternative to hitting the gym, fitness truly becomes a matter of life and death.

A downside pattern repeats: Pushing myself too hard; getting injured or burned out. And, in some ways, fitness is another means to distract me from being a writer.

I have a steady, well-paying job. Working for a small biotech firm in the East Bay.

"A FRONT FOR THE FBI, IT IS," the Booleans assure me as I ride BART through the tunnel under the San Francisco Bay on my way in to work. "IT MAY BE A FAKE COMPANY TO KEEP YOU OCCUPIED RATHER THAN FOCUSING ON THE CONSPIRACY."

Well…so what if it's true? The folks in the office treat me well. My supervisor is a woman named Neise V.

"KNEE-SEE VEE!"

Neise came up from New York and Philadelphia, worked hard all her life. Neise doesn't know about the Boolean Operators—nobody does, really—but she senses something… *unique*…about me. She takes me under her wing, big-sister like. We're quite a pair. A Dominican-American big sister to a Caucasian guy older than she is. Neise teaches me, among other things, not to send an e-mail when I'm so much as the slightest bit angry. It can show through, the anger.

It's great working with Neise and the others, but I don't care for biotech work. Days drag, staring at my computer spreadsheets and poring over mountains of regulatory documents in the file room. 5:00 p.m.: Exhausted in my cubicle; incredible energy spent on a day's work; unable to recall a single thing I accomplished. Obsessing instead over calorie counts, recording every morsel of food consumed in a dietary journal. Marty Diamond's lesson about suicide and regression through past lives is all that's keeping me alive.

One Saturday morning I take my first Krav Maga class. Jeremy Brown is the instructor. If he wasn't teaching Krav, Jeremy would be playing in the NFL or dropping from helicopters as a Navy SEAL. He has speed, strength, and agility that defy most forms of known and speculative science. He played semi-professional soccer in Ecuador while his parents were Missionaries there.

With Jeremy Brown

Seventeen: Krav Maga

My first class, Jeremy runs the dog-pile drill. One student lies on his or her stomach, on the mat. The rest of the students pin him or her down with kicking shields (think of a heavily padded police riot shield). On Jeremy's "Go!" the dog-piled student has to somehow fight to standing and run to safety.

My turn comes.

I lie face-down; the other students form a mini-mountain on top of me.

Part of me, perhaps, is back in Bangkok, when Omar held Thai pads and shouted to throw my round-kicks harder. Or when I was locked up in the psych ward and left those sheriff's deputies no other choice but to pin me down with their padded shields and force me into the jail orange.

"Go!" Jeremy shouts. I struggle to bring my knees to my chest, the way he showed us. The writhing mass of bodies on top of me holds me down.

"Keep fighting!" Jeremy exhorts. The other students are shouting. I bring one knee up, then the other…despite how impossible it seemed a few minutes before, I rise from beneath the dog-pile and make it to safety.

"So," I say to Jeremy after class, "how much are memberships?"

"You had fun, huh?" Jeremy smiles.

With Krav I find something I can channel my energy into.

Something I can do two or three hours a day, five or six days a week.

Maybe it's because when I start Krav, enough time has passed since I quit meth. Maybe there's another reason. Whatever it is, once I take up Krav, most of my suicidal thoughts go away.

Yet my self-discipline remains.

Part of the attraction of Krav, in addition to the heavy emphasis on fitness, is the psychology. The goal of self-defense is not so much to win a fight as it is to *not lose a fight*. How best to accomplish that? Start with a simple calculation: What percentage of fights that we don't get into do we lose? It's the same percentage of weddings I went to when I was smoking meth (zero, to save you flipping back through these pages).

Self-defense lesson: If you're in a knife fight, and you see a finger on the ground, *do not look at your own hand.*

Self-defense lesson (perhaps more practical): Avoid a fight in the first place. It's possible, usually. When it isn't? Krav Maga: brutal counterattacks. Eye gouging, throat punching, groin kicks. A lot of groin kicks. In a "ring fight"—boxing, MMA, Muay Thai, etc.—you're more or less evenly matched against an opponent and given a strict set of rules. On the street? Not the same. It means the self-defense practitioner has to be extra responsible. A Krav Maga counterattack can maim or kill someone. Krav is something you don't want to use, but should there come a time when you need to use it, you don't want to be without it.

"IN SELF-DEFENSE WE HAVE SOMETHING TO DIGEST AND IMPART TO OTHERS."

Sparring classes are Wednesday nights. As I don shin guards and MMA gloves, I steal glances across the training floor at my fellow Krav practitioners. Thomas is putting on his gear, too. He doesn't train very often; I don't know him well. Usually he only shows up Wednesday nights. Although his temper can flare, Thomas' personality is reserved, offbeat, and friendly.

Yet he terrifies me.

Seventeen: Krav Maga

Thomas is overweight. When I was a little kid, a giant bully with rolls of flesh grabbed me on the playground, started spinning me like a human pinwheel. Until I screamed for the teacher to save me. And, of course, Thomas' being overweight reminds me of my own body issues. The other thing about Thomas—his martial arts training gives him the potential to do damage. His lack of control and temper make him a loose cannon. Again, like me.

The one you hate most is the one who is most like you, Donnelly once told me.

Those times I've sparred with Thomas, I've been scared. That he'll kick my knee and rip the ligaments; punch my face and break my nose. Leaving me to have to find something to occupy my dark thoughts other than Krav. As the ring timer sounds and Jeremy shouts at us to hurry up and find partners, I consider those dark thoughts. Suicide, paranoia over the FBI, hopelessness, rage, fear. How much they dominate my life. How they hold me back from doing things to help others. What life might be like without them.

Thomas stands several inches taller than me and at least fifty pounds heavier. I think about the damage he can do with his round kicks, his back fists.

I go over and tap him on the shoulder.

"Hey," I say. "Want to be sparring partners?"

I don't get injured that night.

Survival is success.

From that night on, when we're allowed to choose our own sparring partner, I pick the person I'm most afraid of. Sure, I get hurt from time to time. I learn being hurt is different from being injured. Healing is a skill more so than is it a process. Blood carries nutrients to the overstressed body part; blood carries away toxins. When hurt, it's important to keep the blood flowing. While at the same time avoiding excess strain on the overstressed body part itself. With care and dedication, this is possible. I find I never have to miss a workout due to being hurt, so long as I am careful how I go about that workout.

Many times I leave the gym with a black eye or deep thigh bruise or ringing in my ear. Once I get poked and lose sight in my left eye for a week. My knee pops over and over. I keep getting hit in the same place in my ribs. Yet never once, after falling down, do I fail to force myself to get back up.

Krav…harm and repair; harm and repair.

I pursue a Krav Maga instructor certification. Two nine-day camps spaced six months apart. Eight hours of training each day. The biotech firm generously gives me the time off. I earn my instructor certification. Just barely, and thanks more to the hours I put in, my positive attitude, and the high quality of the teaching of Jeremy Brown and my other instructors, than my skills or abilities. When I pull the black t-shirt with INSTRUCTOR in bold red letters over my head, it's like pulling my sneakers out of the duffle bag that day in Bangkok when Omar first said it was time to make the run. A chance to lead a new life.

I stand before a class of students, beginning to believe the Universe may truly have blessed me with the ability to teach others something about what others have taught me.

In October 2014, the biotech firm's parent company decides to shut down the Oakland office and move operations to New

Seventeen: Krav Maga

Jersey. It's right around the time I earn my Krav instructor certification.

With the suicidal thoughts mostly behind me, with a passion for self-defense driving me, I take the next steps to freedom.

"FREEDOM!"

I leave biotech forever.

Eighteen:
Awards

The cave you fear to enter holds the treasure you seek.

—Joseph Campbell

Biotech and suicidal thoughts are in my rear-view mirror. Like the Nebraska plains behind Mark Burnsen and me in our red Jeep Cherokee, on our cross-country run to where America ends.

"NOW WHO DO WE WISH TO BECOME?"

Quitting drugs is the easy part. The *easier* part, anyway.

The challenge is: how to live a meaningful life without drugs.

During Joe Alioto's campaign, someone had suggested I become a volunteer first responder.

"IT MIGHT BE A GOOD WAY TO GET CLOSER TO THE GOVERNMENT!"

So, I joined the Neighborhood Emergency Response Team (NERT). The San Francisco Fire Department prepares NERT volunteers to assist disaster response services. In the event an earthquake, terrorist attack, tsunami, etc., overwhelms resources. The SFFD trained me: hundreds of hours of basic first aid, search and rescue, triage, scenario drills. I did ride-alongs with the Fire Department paramedics. Along the way, I completed an Emergency Medical Technician course.

I found doctored pictures of myself in the EMT textbook...

"I" attended to accident victims driving a red Jeep Cherokee.

"I" lay unconscious and bleeding after being struck with a baseball.

A NERT scenario takes place on the Presidio. They assemble us in what used to be the Burger King. Near the picture window overlooking the Golden Gate Bridge...where Victor and I ate our last meals before taking to the freedom of the San Francisco nights.

"A KID AGED SIXTEEN! NOT BELIEVING THE GOLDEN GATE BRIDGE WAS NOT ACTUALLY GOLD... UNTIL HE SAW IT WITH HIS OWN EYES."

I continue to endure crushing episodes of FBI conspiracy-fear.

"WE MUST RESOLVE YOUR FBI DILEMMA!"

I'm supposed to do *something* with Omar's story. The question is *what?*

"MAYBE WRITE A BOOK ABOUT IT?"

Indeed. Yet fear paralyzes me. Much of it self-centered, cowardly...people powerful enough to arrange a picture of me in *Sports Illustrated* believe I know too much...cartel mobsters in their employ will overtake me outside my home, smash me into unconsciousness...bind me in the trunk of a car to be driven to an airstrip, loaded on board a plane and flown to a foreign prison, where needles are jabbed into my eyeballs ensure escape is impossible. Decades spend in some dank cellar, until I die from starvation, and my corpse rots away.

It's all self-centered fear...

Ultimately, of course, Omar was my friend.

There's no proof he was anyone other than whom he claimed. *Yet that picture in Sports Illustrated is of me...the Omsex picture...the Perpendicular Planes...*

Omar was a Mossad agent, or with the French intelligence or CIA. Were our enemies to find out, tides of sentiment would turn against our allies; innocent people would fall victim.

"*Never let the enemy know to what extent it was infiltrated,*" I read somewhere.

The FBI will contact me, when enough time has passed so it's safe for the public to know the truth...

"YOU YOURSELF ARE AN UNDERCOVER OPERATIVE, AFTER ALL."

Yet these things are what the schizophrenic believes too, right?

It's just a matter of time before the FBI shows up at my front door to inform me my role in the counterterrorism war-game is over. My contributions have helped protect innocents. No one would put pictures of me in *Sports Illustrated* or EMT textbooks, follow me with Perpendicular Planes, or give me the Boolean Operators...unless it was for something good.

I was a drug addict, yes. Committed many crimes.

Terrorism, treason, anything related? Were not among them.

"THEREFORE, YOU MUST BE AN UNDERCOVER OPERATIVE!"

The players smash forth on their one-wheeled contraptions... there are never any injuries, no lasting forms of trauma. Not in the Cellar Hole.

And, of course, we can't ignore the distinct possibility Omar was simply whom he claimed...

"BUT THAT SEEMS IMPOSSIBLE."

Eighteen: Awards

Exposing him to public scrutiny would cause him harm. And already, much prejudice and hatred has been directed against Muslims. They've suffered more than enough. Wouldn't the musings of a former meth addict, that a Muslim man who *looked a little* like Satam al Suqami had anything to do with terrorists, simply add to their suffering?

As simple as it may sound, when the fear consumes me, I turn to God. If God wants me in prison, kidnapped, or dead… these are places I'll go. Not *happily*, to be sure. But spirituality can lead a person from some very dark places. Like the ancient saint said, *"All the darkness in the world can't extinguish the light of a single candle."*

Without the fear, there may never have come a search for spiritual meaning.

Still, I often feel like a terrible person…I've let down the American public. Especially those who lost people close to them—they deserve to know the truth behind why.

"BECAUSE YOU BELIEVED ONE OF THE HIJACKERS WAS AN INFILTRATOR YET SAID NOTHING PUBLICLY ABOUT IT."

Yes.

"LIKE YOU'RE IN ON THE CONSPIRACY."

Yes…

"LIKE YOU'RE GIVING TACIT ENDORSEMENT."

Yes!

If one of the hijackers was indeed a counterterrorism infiltrator living in Bangkok in late 2000, it's up to the public, not me, to decide if it *is meaningful*. But the public *can't* decide because the public doesn't have the information.

I have the information.
I haven't made enough progress in figuring out who Omar really was...
I can never bring my *best self* to the world.

The priority is protecting intended victims of terrorism.
I've contacted authorities many times...if, like the Boolean Operators have often claimed, Omar was a terrorist, this is the right thing to do, certainly.

If, like the Boolean Operators have also claimed, he was working for the French, or the Mossad, it stands to reason the counterterrorism authorities wish this to remain a secret.

"YOU ARE BEST SERVING COUNTERTERRORISM BY KEEPING OMAR'S STORY PRIVATE."

Of course, if Omar was an undercover operative, an infiltrator? Then, naturally, he—and the people he worked for, who must be involved in counterterrorism—would want his cover story maintained.

"AN INFILTRATOR WOULD WISH TO BE TREATED LIKE A TERRORIST! THE FBI HAS HYPNOTICALLY TRAINED YOU TO KNOW SO."

It's a twisted maze of a guessing game, one that's found me far, far less than heroic...paralyzed with fright...the ramifications of the wrong move, spinning the mind's wheels until they smoke.

What could I possibly have that you might want to read about?

Eighteen: Awards

Date: September 28, 2014
From: Peter "Ed" Kressy
To: Senator Dianne Feinstein
Subject: Inquiry to Office of Sen. Feinstein

Dear Senator Feinstein;

Greetings from San Francisco! When I first came here in 1986, I lived very near your home on Presidio Terrace.

I write to ask your advice, in your capacity as Chair of the Senate Select Committee on Intelligence, regarding the following:

It is quite possible that a former associate of mine, (Omar), was/was affiliated with a terrorist, Satam al Suqami. This goes back to November–December 2000, in Bangkok, Thailand. (Omar) and I met while we were students at a Muay Thai school there.

I have provided what information I have to the U.S. authorities.

(Omar's) possible affiliation with Suqami has been confirmed by a friend of a friend of mine, who is a former high-ranking official of a federal law enforcement entity. My question relates to whether I should move forward with attempts to make this information public.

Among my concerns, of course, is that to do so might inadvertently hamper the efforts of those involved in counterterrorism. I once read that it is not advisable to ever let the enemy (terrorists, in this case) know to what extent it has been infiltrated (or investigated, etc.) Seems to make sense, but how does one balance this against the American public's right to information?

What I am asking, is: Assume, for argument's sake, a connection between (Omar) and Satam al Suqami. How does the U.S.

Intelligence Community wish for me to act/not act upon this information?

Any guidance that you might be so kind as to provide, is greatly appreciated.

Thank you.

Date: September 30, 2014
From: "Buchwald, Mike (Intelligence)"
To: Peter "Ed" Kressy
Subject: Re: Inquiry to Office of Sen. Feinstein

Dear Mr. Kressy,

Thank you for writing Senator Feinstein. I am on her Intelligence Committee staff and I write to respond to your September 28th email (below).

Without knowing more about the specifics of your allegations, we can't make any independent judgments on what should made public and what should not, but, of course, you should not publicly state anything that may be classified.

You said you have provided information to the "U.S. authorities." Does that mean you have provided that information to the FBI? Whoever you have talked to is most likely closer to the investigation and may be in a better position to advise you. However, if there is any information you wish to provide to the U.S. Intelligence Community, I would be happy to pass along that information—or your questions—to the FBI or another part of the Intelligence Community if applicable.

Eighteen: Awards

Please let me know how you think we can best help answer your question.

Sincerely,

Mike Buchwald

Senate Select Committee on Intelligence

211 Hart Office Building

Washington D.C. 20510

Date: October 1, 2014
From: Peter "Ed" Kressy
To: "Buchwald, Mike (Intelligence)"
Subject: Re: Inquiry to Office of Sen. Feinstein

Dear Mr. Buchwald;

Many thanks for your message. To answer your question: Yes, I have provided what information I have to the FBI.

I appreciate your offer to pass along information to the U.S. Intelligence Community. Attached please find a letter to the Senate Select Committee on Intelligence, as well as several photos taken in Bangkok, Thailand in November–December 2000. I am the American wearing the beard, who appears in all but one of the photos. (Omar) is the man seen in all photos; it is he who may have been/been affiliated with the terrorist Satam al Suqami.

It may be that (Omar) may have somehow been working for an entity that was part of, or friendly towards, the U.S. (i.e., as an "undercover" or informant). This is only a theory and cannot be proven with the information I have.

Feel free to pass along the attached as per the needs and interests of the U.S. Intelligence Community.

As to your statement about how you can best help answer my question: Can you confirm that I have done all that needs to be done, as far as helping the U.S. Intelligence Community? If not, what else is there that I can do to help? I understand from your message that I should not publicly state anything which may be classified.

Please let me know if you have any questions or if additional information is needed.

Thanks again.

Ed

Date: October 6, 2014
From: "Buchwald, Mike (Intelligence)"
To: Peter "Ed" Kressy
Subject: Re: Inquiry to Office of Sen. Feinstein

Mr. Kressy,

Pursuant to your request, I have forwarded the materials to the FBI that you sent so that they can be reviewed by the U.S. Intelligence Community.

Thank you again for writing Sen. Feinstein.

Sincerely,

Mike Buchwald

Eighteen: Awards

Date: October 7, 2014
From: Peter "Ed" Kressy
To: "Buchwald, Mike (Intelligence)"
Subject: Re: Inquiry to Office of Sen. Feinstein

Dear Mr. Buchwald,

Many thanks again for your assistance. I will consult with you before initiating further actions, or responding to inquiries from the public, regarding this matter.

Best,
Ed

"THUS, YOU BROUGHT THE STORY OF OMAR TO THE ATTENTION OF THE HIGHEST AUTHORITY IN THE LAND, ISN'T THAT RIGHT?"

Indeed. It would seem Mike Buchwald's contacts are at or near the highest levels in the FBI. His messages give me confidence…no matter what terrible things I may imagine the FBI has in store for me… When I approach the real FBI in a spirit of trust and cooperation, I feel I'm doing something to help protect innocent people. The feeling is a rock I can anchor myself to.

I need that anchor. Paranoia and doubt form a storm swirling about…

There's a line in my email:

(Omar's) possible affiliation with al Suqami has been confirmed by a friend of a friend of mine, who is a former high-ranking official of a federal law enforcement entity.

"THIS IS TRUE ENOUGH!"

Indeed...the "evidence" in my email was *factually true*. But the *conclusions* I let myself come to were conclusions my mind had already arrived at, before the evidence appeared.

Mike Buchwald's line gives me great pause:

...but, of course, you should not publicly state anything that may be classified.

Certainly, I've never been given any classified information.

"OR HAVE WE?"

Could the United States Intelligence Community have transferred classified knowledge to me via subliminal messaging, through HyperSonic Sound?

Is my "knowledge," knowledge which "may be classified"?

"DO WE TRULY HAVE CLASSIFIED KNOWLEDGE?"

I don't feel it's my place to ask Mike Buchwald what he means, or to press him further to answer my questions. I've pushed far enough...I'm a former meth addict—someone hated so much they put pictures of me in *Sports Illustrated*, hoping I'll kill myself. My family and friends all got on board. They all wanted me dead, or at least shamed into silence.

"THEY TRAINED YOU TO BE AN UNDERCOVER OPERATIVE!"

I'm not confident in putting forward the idea Omar may have been an undercover operative, much beyond using vague language like "possible affiliation with a terrorist" rather than "may have been a terrorist." That and my one simple paragraph:

> It may be that (Omar) may have somehow been working for an entity that was part of, or friendly towards, the U.S. (i.e., as an

Eighteen: Awards

"undercover" or informant). This is only a theory and cannot be proven with the information I have.

(Note: the above paragraph originally appeared in the letter I attached to the email, not the email itself. The edit is made in the interests of brevity.)

"ONE SEEMS NEVER CERTAIN WHOM OR WHAT TO TRUST."

No. I'm supposed to know what Mike Buchwald means, without having to ask.

And, the only "evidence" Omar had anything to do with the hijackers?

Is also evidence I am schizophrenic.

Episodes of earth-shaking paranoia make me believe Mike Buchwald's emails are a trick. That I'll be set up for passing along classified information.

Life in prison…executed for treason.

But those are delusions.

Today, I realize…

The story isn't so much about whether or not Omar was other than whom he claimed.

The story is about how we can overcome our fears, turn our lives around.

What could I possibly have that you might want to read about?

In November 2014, I'm teaching regular classes for KMI.

Elliot is one of my students.

He's also an FBI SWAT team agent.

"COINCIDENCE?"

The FBI SWAT team! The very ones I've been so afraid would kick down my door, drag me away. But if I'm going to get better—really better—I have to face my fears.

Elliot knows I volunteer for NERT…

"I'd like to volunteer for the FBI, too," I tell him after a noon combat cardio class. "Do you ever need role-players, you know, in hostage rescue scenarios, or something?"

He throws a few combinations against a heavy bag. The chains rattle as it swings from the ceiling. Elliot was in an elite military fighting unit and played football for a Big Ten school.

"You know what," he says, "would you be interested in leading a Krav Maga session for our SWAT team?"

For weeks, we exchange emails. Setting agendas, drafting plans.

March 25, 2015: I'm riding my bicycle to KMI, stopped at a red light. Near where a small circle of tents, serving as shelter for homeless people, stands a few feet from zooming freeway vehicles. My backpack falls out of the handlebar wire basket, thudding onto the pavement. My drink mixture—water, apple cider vinegar, chia seeds—inside, in a glass bottle. The bottle breaks, and everything—including my San Francisco Police Department baseball cap—is soaked in apple cider vinegar with chia seeds stuck everywhere. The cap was a gift from a retired SFPD officer, one of my Krav students. It's part of the official police uniform.

In the windowless KMI bathroom, I clean my cap as best I can. It's pretty messed up but by no means ruined. Hopefully, it won't start sprouting and make me look like an SFPD-sponsored Chia Pet. Anyway, there's no time to worry about it…

Elliot and his FBI SWAT team arrive.

Eighteen: Awards

And soon afterwards, Rory Miller shows up.

On a trip to visit my parents in Massachusetts, at the Toadstool Bookstore in Peterborough, New Hampshire, I found a lone copy of Rory's book *Facing Violence*. Soon I discovered: Rory's a guy who, if you spend any amount of time in a serious study of self-defense, you'll probably hear about.

Rory—a lifelong martial artist—interacted with many violent inmates. When he was with a sheriff's department outside of Portland, Oregon. He understands martial arts' practical applications to real-life violence and the psychology behind keeping oneself safe. He's written many books and teaches around the world, including at Soja Studios in Oakland (now moved to Berkeley), where I attend his seminars.

Rory takes certain self-defense instructors under his wing. I'm fortunate enough to be one of them. I apply myself to Rory's work, like I did with Joe Alioto and Sebastian. They believe in me. I start believing in myself.

Rory's in town for a Soja seminar the weekend after the SWAT team training. He's agreed to teach the FBI guys. On March 25, 2015, I'm standing next to Rory Miller, a person I would never have met back in my meth days.

Wearing my shirt with INSTRUCTOR in red letters that I never would've had the chance to wear had I not been given help to quit meth.

Facing a cadre of real FBI SWAT team persons—the same persons who I'd been so desperately afraid of—as their teacher.

D___ is one of those guys, a SWAT team lead. After ninety minutes or so of training with Rory, D___ comes up to me. "Ed," he says, clapping me on the back, "that was great. Thank you so much for setting this up." I'll train D___ and Elliot a couple other times. So, thanks to Krav Maga, Rory, and a lot of other people and things, I've made my first friends in the FBI.

D___ will nominate me for the FBI Citizens Academy.

Law enforcement persons and I have clashed. Police officers have searched my home and vehicle, stripped me naked, and locked me in a safety cell…

Law enforcement persons have been very good to me.

One night when I was a resident at the Ohlhoff House, Nathaniel showed up to talk to us. He spoke about recovery, about turning our lives around. Nate was a police officer but was at the House on his own time. Not only that but on subsequent nights, he returned to the Ohlhoff House—to pick up three of us residents, bring us into his own home and coach us on turning our lives around. We were three guys pretty much right off the streets…one of us had recently robbed a McDonald's with a shotgun. Can you imagine, an off-duty cop bringing three guys like us *into his home?*

Yet it's what Nathaniel did.

He—like my friend Two Jacks, from jail—didn't have to go out of his way to help me.

But that's what Nathaniel and Two Jacks did.

They taught me that to seek the humanity of the person behind a uniform—whether the uniform of a prisoner, or a police officer—is to find humanity within myself.

Towards the end of 2015, I discover Defy Ventures.

For years I've been participating in Toastmasters, the speechmaking organization. I'm a member of the Rhino Business

Eighteen: Awards

Toastmasters, founded by local legend Jinsoo Terry. Jinsoo was a successful business executive in Korea before she came to America and launched a practice training cross-cultural communication and diversity in the workplace. San Francisco Mayor Willie Brown proclaimed July 10, 2001 as "Jinsoo Terry Day."

The Rhino club serves dinner before meetings. When I was smoking meth, I showed up just to eat for free. Once, I gobbled down Chinese food and left before the meeting even started.

The club elects me "Sergeant-at-Arms." My job includes arriving early to set up and staying late to clean up. Still stir-crazy even years after the meth, when the meetings near the finish and I can't sit still, I clear plates and cups. Like a restaurant busser. Everyone thinks I'm being proactive…at the end of the term, they recognize me with the "Jinsoo Terry Award" for the member who contributes the most.

Public speaking always terrified me. Most forms of communication did. Yet I force myself to stand before the Rhino crash (a "crash" is to rhinos as "pride" is to lions) and talk. I may never get to the point of being an exceptional speechmaker. But I develop confidence in myself, thanks to the Rhino's support. Many nights after a meeting, I've shaken hands all around with my Rhino colleagues, then gone smiling outside, striding down the stairs to the BART station…stood up straight at the platform as trains shot through the underground tube, and thought to myself: *I've just spent a few hours with some of the nicest, finest people in the world.*

I deliver speeches on how I overcame addiction, served some time in jail. Stefanie Chow is a Rhino who goes on to lead the Toastmasters District Four, all clubs from San Francisco to Palo Alto. Stefanie will introduce me to Ernest Kirkwood, an incredible human being who served almost three decades in prison and now assists many others to successfully reenter society following incarceration. Ernest speaks, and wisdom pours from his lips like rainwater down a mountain stream after a thunderstorm high at the summit above. Ernest enrolls me in starting a Toastmasters-style club in a women's unit of county jail. As I write this, we continue to convene the "Breadwinners" club every Thursday. We've brought in numerous guest speakers from Toastmasters clubs, public service agencies, and businesses. The women of Breadwinners deliver speeches of their own, of course. As they do, they learn how to better advocate for themselves and plan to return to productive members of society.

Stefanie Chow also introduces me to someone who introduces me to Seth Sundberg.

Seth played backup center to Shaquille O'Neal on the Lakers. Like the old saws about going from Park Avenue to the park bench, from Penn State to the State Pen, Seth went from NBA hardwood to doing hard time. While serving five years for tax fraud, Seth worked in the prison kitchen. One day he hoisted a box of chicken from a storeroom shelf, only to see it clearly labeled "not for human consumption." Soon after, he taught himself to make granola bars from items from the prison commissary. Upon release, he launched "Prison Bars," a "criminally delicious snack bar" through Defy Ventures' program.

Catherine "Cat" Hoke founded Defy Ventures, a nonprofit that delivers training in entrepreneurship, employment, and character development to currently and formerly incarcerated men and women. Cat left a Manhattan career in venture capital after volunteering in prison alongside Chuck Colson (Colson was the former special counsel to Richard Nixon—served prison time for his role in Watergate, and later founded the nonprofit ministry Prison Fellowship).

Cat may have intended to teach incarcerated persons, but they taught her...incarcerated persons often have entrepreneurial skills, which, when applied to legitimate business ventures, allow them another avenue to successful reentry to society. For a returning citizen (a person reentering society following incarceration), owning a business can make more sense than being an employee. The theory being, employers care about an applicant's past...yet when it comes to the person selling a product or providing a service? The customer cares more who he or she is *today*.

Imagine a woodcutter, shouldering his ax and venturing into the forest. Intending to fell a tree, for lumber to build his family's home, firewood to warm it and cook food over. The woodcutter happens upon a perfect specimen, a tall and mighty tree. Yet instead of chopping it down, he exclaims: "This tree is not worth considering...one hundred years ago, it was only a sapling!"

It's ridiculous, of course.

But how many opportunities do we as a society deny our returning citizens based upon their pasts? Like the long-ago sapling offers value as the mighty tree it is today, so do those human beings have who made mistakes, paid their debts, and turned their lives around.

I join Defy Ventures' program, becoming an Entrepreneur-in-Training (EIT).

As I work closely with returning citizens who deserve second chances, I believe I deserve a second chance, too. I believe I can find a way to contribute to the world beyond a career in biotech.

Mike Gaudio and the company he works for are big Defy supporters. Mike, despite his busy days as a manager at Google, finds time to be my executive mentor. He spends countless hours helping me launch a corporate self-defense training business. Basic self-defense mindsets and principles, as a learning exercise and team-building activity. It works, believe it or not. Clients hire me: Cisco, Google, LinkedIn, Slack, and others. These companies get value from my services. But it would almost impossible for me to become their vendor, were it not for Defy. It says a lot about these organizations, of the many fine individuals who wish to be hired by them; these companies give me a chance because I am with Defy.

Mike Gaudio mentors me as I pursue my dream of writing this book.

He believes in me. As a result, I further believe in myself.

Mike's company gives me much assistance, too. Google people make a video for me to promote my business, take meetings with me to advise my work, bring me in to speak at an event. The feeling from a firm as successful as Google taking a chance on me gives me impetus to continue serving my communities.

Cat Hoke and Defy Ventures end up going their separate ways. I continue to support them both—volunteering inside prisons, attending post-release program events, advocating

Eighteen: Awards

for them where I can. Thanks to the exceptional individuals I encounter through Defy, Google, Rhino, and elsewhere, I come to understand: helping others overcome their obstacles helps me overcome mine.

"SO, WHAT OTHER OBSTACLES ARE LEFT TO SURMOUNT?"

My first application to the FBI Citizens Academy gets turned down. Even with D___ as my sponsor.

The second time I apply, same thing.

My third application is turned down.

Paranoid fears mount and remount. I worry the FBI is playing some sort of psychological game. Letting the hammer slowly, tortuously drop. I fall out of touch with D___. I panic, sending him long, unnecessary text messages. When I don't hear from him, I think I've blown my chance.

Yet I persevere. I continue to reach out. I send D___ short texts on holidays, wishing him well.

Finally, on Thanksgiving Day 2017…seventeen years after I sat down to Thanksgiving Dinner at the Karnmanee Palace hotel, and eleven years after I asked the Boolean Operators to marry me…I get a message from D___.

We're still on. He remains willing to sponsor me for the Citizens Academy.

Date: December 2, 2017
From: Peter "Ed" Kressy
To: "Buchwald, Mike (Intelligence)"
Subject: Re: Inquiry to Office of Sen. Feinstein

Dear Mr. Buchwald;

I hope this message finds you well. Regarding the matter about which we corresponded, I had an idea to run by you: I wish to research 9/11 victims' advocacy groups and forward my information to someone who might use it to help victims and their loved ones.
Of course, my primary goal is to help the Intelligence Community prevent people from being victims of terrorism. With that in mind, do you have any suggestions? If I do not hear back by 12/9, I will decide how/if to move forward. Regardless, I will follow your previous advice.

Thank you as always for all your assistance, much appreciated.

Date: December 2, 2017
From: postmaster@mac.com
To: Peter "Ed" Kressy
Subject: Re: Inquiry to Office of Sen. Feinstein

This report relates to a message you sent: Your message cannot be delivered.
Reason: Remote server has rejected address
User Unknown

Eighteen: Awards

It isn't the first time I'd raised the possibility of making Omar's story public with Mike Buchwald. But various fears choked me out. Now that Mike's moved on from his role in the Senate (as the email bounce-back suggests) I feel free to decide what, if anything, to do with Omar's story.

I never end up doing much research into 9/11 victims' advocacy groups, as I'd mentioned to Mike Buchwald. I lack faith in myself…in my mind I'm still perceived by others as delusional, not to be trusted.

"YET WE MUST FIND THE PROPER WAY TO MAKE THIS STORY PUBLIC!"

In December 2017, I get the chance to have a conversation with the well-known and highly respected Seth Godin. We're riding together in a shuttle van to a Defy Ventures event. The two-day event takes some of us Entrepreneurs-in-Training on a tour of Silicon Valley businesses, to meet leaders such as Sheryl Sandberg and Jeff Weiner, CEO of LinkedIn (one of our EITs inadvertently calls Sandberg by a wrong first name, giving Defy Ventures a likely first within the offices of Facebook).

I don't remember exactly what Seth Godin told me—I do remember he imparted a great deal of compassionate wisdom to all us EITs, through the course of those two days—but it was like he telepathically implanted an idea in my head.

"THAT SEEMS AN ODD WAY TO COMMUNICATE."

The next day, I get up at four in the morning, meditate, turn on my laptop, and start turning Seth's implanted idea into this book.

In January 2018, I see a movie called *The Post*. About *The Washington Post's* decision to publish materials related to the

Pentagon Papers, despite the potential consequences, which seemed dire. That movie, combined with confidence inspired by D___, Elliot, and Mike Buchwald, inspire me to find the courage to begin bringing Omar's story to the public. I start making inquiries to retired FBI agents, lawyers, professors. Remaining clear there's no proof whatsoever Omar was anything other than a French kickboxer.

The fear remains.

Constant, crushing at times...

The FBI is going to smash down my door, send me to prison for life, employ gangsters to murder me.

Yet in April 2018, the FBI...the *real* FBI...accepts me to their Citizens Academy.

The Citizens Academy is part of the FBI's Community Outreach program. According to the Bureau's website, it is designed to "...give business, religious, civic, and community leaders an inside look at the FBI. The mission...is to foster a greater understanding of the role of federal law enforcement in the community through frank discussion and education."

"YOU COULD BENEFIT FROM A GREATER UNDERSTANDING OF THE ROLE OF FEDERAL LAW ENFORCEMENT! WE WILL FACILITATE YOUR LEARNING."

The first class is on a Tuesday evening. I spend the day waiting for an email to arrive telling me it has all been a mistake. The email never arrives; the Academy begins.

My fellow students are in security roles with tech companies, working in public safety, serving as representatives of Muslim

Eighteen: Awards

communities. One leads a nonprofit that serves victims of human trafficking and sexual exploitation. We students spend a night a week for six weeks learning about counterterrorism, economic espionage, and organized crime. Agents show us techniques for evidence collection, educate us on how the Bureau builds cases against public corruption.

The Academy gives me the opportunity to contribute to the FBI's helping victims...of crime, yes, and of our own mistakes. I'll go on to work with the Bureau to better serve the reentry community (persons released from incarceration and their supporters) and combat the opioid epidemic. I'll speak at a showing of *Chasing the Dragon*, a film the FBI and DEA created to raise awareness of the opioid epidemic.

Much of my work is the simple act of speaking well about the Bureau, recognizing their commitment to giving second chances. Finding opportunities to write about triumph over FBI fears.

What could I possibly have that you might want to read about?

Few people, I imagine, have greater reason to fear the FBI than did I. My fears were all in my mind, of course, but they were as real to me as the words on this page, as the characters from the Cellar Hole.

"AS REAL AS THE VOICES YOU'RE HEARING NOW!"

The FBI allowing me to participate in the Citizens Academy has an important benefit.

Soon after the Citizens Academy begins, all but a few vestiges of my FBI paranoia go away.

No longer do I fear the FBI will set me up for life in prison, or assassinate me.

I discuss Omar with several FBI agents and employees...

All of whom I'm grateful to, for giving me the confidence to write this story.

By no means do I intend a blanket endorsement of any law enforcement entity. But it would be unfair for me not to clearly state: Were it not for the FBI admitting me to the Citizens Academy, I don't know I would've found the courage to tell you about Omar.

Thank you FBI...thank you Mike Buchwald, and your Senate Select Committee on Intelligence. As your emails demonstrate, when I reached out to you, you treated me with fairness and respect. You made me believe I was accomplishing what I set out to do: protect innocent people. I debated a great deal whether to include our emails in this book. Ultimately I did so in order to show that by overcoming my addiction and extreme paranoia, and approaching you in a spirit of putting innocent persons' needs first, I found success. Hopefully others will be inspired to do the same.

Thank you, all our sisters and brothers who are/were incarcerated and are turning your lives around. For inspiring me, for giving me courage, belief in myself...for setting an example, of how by changing myself I may bring positive change to the world around me.

Was Satam al Suqami a counterterrorism infiltrator? Does the story of my friend Omar shed any more light on the tragic events of 9/11?

If Omar was an infiltrator, hopefully a balance is struck: In light of the public's right to know, enough time has passed to

Eighteen: Awards

make it safe to tell his story.

It's worth repeating: To be clear, it's highly unlikely I would've thought Omar had anything to do with the terrorists, had it not been for the Boolean Operators, the gaslighting.

If the pictures in *Sports Illustrated*, etc., were of me...if the Perpendicular Planes and the rest were real...then yes, there is probably something about Omar's story that reveals more about 9/11. You'd have to believe those things (*Sports Illustrated,* etc.) to believe Omar was other than he claimed.

But I did believe them. And much more.

My beliefs once made me afraid...very afraid.

Remarkable people and organizations inspired me to overcome my fears.

"THIS IS WHAT OMAR'S STORY IS ABOUT!"

Of course, it could be both that I'm schizophrenic *and* there are pictures of me in magazines and textbooks...

How would it be if my friend Omar *had been* Satam al Suqami...

Of course, in no way would I consider him to have truly been my friend if he had been an actual terrorist.

"BUT, LIKE YOU, HE WAS AN UNDERCOVER OPERATIVE."

The tough thing would be thinking of the families of the 9/11 victims. For all these years, there would've been information they didn't have. Information I *did* have. And made the decision not to tell them.

The tough thing would be a Muslim man was heroically working undercover—ultimately sacrificing his life—to fight terrorism...and the world hasn't known.

And…if my friend Omar *hadn't been* Suqami?

He's alive today, probably, and I pray he's doing well…

Maybe he's reading this.

Maybe he's still making the run somewhere…

And somehow motioning for me to keep up, keep up…

To run faster, to do better.

It took me a long time to bring Omar's story to light. Perhaps too long. It's been tempting, very tempting, to let it go, allow the story fade into nothingness…pretend none of it happened.

But that doesn't seem fair.

People affected by 9/11 deserve to know the truth. Muslims, and families and friends of the victims. Omar's story is yours as much as mine—perhaps more so.

Sure, I've considered your perspectives—yet much of my thinking has been self-centered. *Will Muslims blame me for my poor choices leading to psychosis, my ensuing beliefs Omar might've had something to do with terrorists—my contacting authorities about what I believed?*

Will families of 9/11 victims blame me for not having done enough?

I would probably blame me, if I were you.

I believed in the Boolean Operators, the gaslighting.

"WHERE IS THE DIFFERENCE BETWEEN TRUE REALITY AND THE CERTAINTY SOMETHING IS REAL?"

Fortunately, the people in my life inspired me to tell the truth, insofar as I know it.

Despite how long it took.

And, of course, to Omar from Bangkok…

Eighteen: Awards

I defended you as best I could, despite what the Boolean Operators and my psychosis told me. I clung to a belief you were a counterterrorism operative…that things went wrong beyond your control. You befriended me—even if you were doing so undercover—in a country foreign to us both, during one of the longest stretches I'd gone without meth in a long time.

There's been a lot of fear as I write this book.

Fear I took too long to write it…

Made too many mistakes along the way…

Fear I failed to bring the evidence I believed was real to the public. To you.

Fear others will retaliate against me for having offended them.

Fear the FBI will silence me, with prison or death.

Fear is like fire.

It can warm our home; it can burn our house down.

I let fear burn my house down.

I lived in an empty stone foundation.

I cry on the school bus…afraid I'll never get back to my Cellar Hole.

I rip the home on Monterey Boulevard to pieces…

This book is my attempt to build a new home.

I sat with my bedbugs in my North Beach SRO, feeling sorry for myself.

Many times I did that.

I'd lie on my mattress crying. Begging the Boolean Operators not to leave me. Longing for Mickey and the home on Monterey Boulevard. Hating myself for having thrown it all away.

"YOU DIDN'T THROW EVERYTHING AWAY.

YOU KEPT US!"

The Boolean Operators are likely in my life to stay. To explain their presence now: Imagine staring at a light bulb. You look away, and you see an image...a blob of purple or green or orange, there in your field of vision. You *see that image,* yes. But you see it for what it is, and not without first staring at your light bulb.

The Boolean Operators are with me when I want them to be. It can be rather solitary, the life of an attempting-to-be-a-writer. As I weave a path through telling a story like Omar's, the Boolean Operators seem worthy of a love I can imagine one reserves for a spouse.

"WE ARE HAPPY AS YOUR SPOUSE! AND YOU ARE INDEED A WRITER."

Yet Boolean Operators or not...through my recovery, when the time came for me to be somewhere, *I was there.*

Joe Alioto's campaign headquarters, the Bay Club hardwood with Bryan, Tigers' Cave, Krav Maga class, setting up the room for a Rhino Toastmasters meeting. I am fortunate for so many people in my life. *I had to not let them down.*

Despite crushing doubt and uncertainty, I put one foot in front of the other.

Because of the people in my life.

Others' examples taught me to work very hard at working hard; force myself to show up. Boolean Operators in tow; conspiracy theories swirling. Nearly always unsure of myself; hardly ever in possession of the confidence it seemed everyone else had plenty of which to spare.

Resentments—of people and circumstances—strangled

Eighteen: Awards

me. But resentments are like drinking poison and hoping *my enemies* die. When times came to make public expressions…in conversations, emails, statements…I strove to show appreciation. Erica and Joe Alioto, and many others, taught me to let the percentage of myself that appreciates others be the percentage I turned outwards.

The way you treat others is the way you treat yourself.

Eventually—it took years—my words and actions changed what was in my heart and mind. Thanks to the many amazing people in my life, I've learned—slowly, painfully—to fight against the self-indulgent patterns of thinking of myself and others as "less than."

To instead follow a path of self-improvement.

For years, I'm rising before dawn almost every day…first to meditate, then to write. Even though I can't believe I should be a success, can't believe I might be worth setting after my dream. Leaving biotech carried with it a great deal of uncertainty. The equivalent of a six-figure salary, the close-to-guaranteed availability of work. Despite having been unhappy, the level of comfort I found in the cubicles and conference rooms is very hard to escape.

Comfort does not equal happiness.

"WHAT DOES EQUAL HAPPINESS?"

I enter the FBI headquarters on May 3, 2019. My name appears in lights on a screen, along with the names of the fifty-six other Americans being recognized with the Director's Community Leadership Award (DCLA). An hour later, I'm shaking hands with Christopher Wray, FBI director, as he presents me my award.

The Bureau is recognizing my work with Defy Ventures, the Breadwinners Toastmasters-style club, the NERT program, FBI outreach initiatives... I like to think, too, they award me the DCLA to show appreciation of persons who overcome addiction and fear and try to help others do the same. Thanks to the faith in myself instilled in me by the Bureau—and many others—I've shed the skin of my past self and truly become someone new.

"YOU SEE? YOU REALLY WERE AN UNDERCOVER OPERATIVE! YOUR OLD SELF WAS LIKE YOUR DISGUISE."

Thanks to the FBI, we know: if one person with a history of drug addiction/criminality (me) can rise to be recognized by the director of the principal law enforcement entity in America, others can, too.

By recognizing me, the FBI further proves second chances are worth giving.

Few people, I imagine, have greater reason to fear the FBI than I did...my fears were as real to me as the characters from the Cellar Hole.

In my world, never in the history of the Bureau have more resources been employed to disrupt the life of an innocent individual—me. Largely innocent, anyway...all along I knew: *I was not guilty.* Not of terrorism, espionage, etc. Still, my psychosis, the gaslighting, paralyzed me. Of course, the FBI was never going to approach me, or call it off...why would they? It was the *Boolean FBI* behind it all. Yet when I found the strength to approach the *real* FBI in the spirit of what I could

Eighteen: Awards

offer our common interests of improving society, I found my forms of redemption.

The same day I enter FBI headquarters, an article I write about the DCLA is published in *The Washington Post*. The night before, I'd been given a tour of The Post's newsroom. Even got a chance to meet Marty Baron, the managing editor. My article concludes: *"Today, one of the least likely people to be receiving a community service award from the director of the FBI will indeed receive it. And let me tell you with extreme certainty: If someone like me can come this far, in your life, anything is possible too."*

With Cat Hoke, founder of Defy Ventures (photo courtesy of Defy Ventures)

From FBI Website: Receiving Community Service Award from Christopher Wray, FBI Director

Nineteen:

Families

"*I tell you, my friends, do not be afraid of those who kill the body and after that can do no more.*"

—Luke 12:4

I fly to see family. I like to fly. It's unnatural. Flying is unnatural, that is. Who designed a human being to zip along at hundreds of miles an hour? Through a place in space where air is so thin, no human could survive?

"WHO COULD SURVIVE UP THERE?"

But I like leaving home for the airport at a pre-dawn hour, which, back in the meth days, would find me cowering in my black leather armchair or screaming at the cutout eye sockets in my Excelsior studio walls. I enjoy taking BART south to the airport instead of north/east to my old biotech job.

I prefer the unusual heaviness of my backpack as I hoist it over my shoulders—even though it's stuffed with only enough clothes for four days and I'll be away for longer (when going to see family, you have the chance to do laundry). The backpack also holds running shoes, a laptop, the most recent *New Yorker* magazines…snacks, of course. Clif Bars, cashews, chocolate.

"THE THREE C'S OF AIRLINE TRAVEL!"

Nineteen: Families

Of course, it rarely contains a gift for whatever family I'm going to see...I usually forget to pick something up.

But my family forgives me.

My cousins in Portland, Salt Lake City, and the small town down the California coast. Blossom out to the east. And, of course, my parents, who still live down the hill from the Welcome to Ashburnham sign on the giant water tower. My beautiful, wonderful family has helped me, perhaps most of all. Although I hurt them as much as, if not more than, myself, they took me back in. They inspire me to do the hard work to become a better person.

The meth, the other drugs, were killing my heart, killing the rest of my body. The assassins I believed stalked me were out to put blades and bullets through my heart. Yet any power the drugs and phantom assassins had was to kill my body. After that, they could do no more.

The true danger came from the rest...the Boolean Operators, before I quit meth and learned to live with them, even love them. The terror of the FBI, before I was shown how to overcome it and become grateful to the Bureau. The danger came from secrets I kept about Omar, kept about my schizophrenia-like condition...*we're only as sick as our secrets*, as they say in the 12-step meetings...secrets which I learned, as I wrote about them, have the power to heal.

Before I learned how to transform them, those things had the power to kill my soul.

I love my Uncle Jupiter. My cousin Lynn, too—all my family. I've learned those times when my family members *fail to suit me*—like almost every time when people and circumstances don't suit me—it's *me* who needs to change. Become a better nephew, cousin, brother. Even if I'm *thinking about* my own selfish desires, I don't have to *act like* I am. I can strive to do the honest, right things...despite any personal loss I may perceive as coming as a result, or any personal gain I believe might come from doing the opposite. I can instead consider: how do I give others what my family has given me?

Throughout this book I've written about spirituality. Although certainly not as much as I've *thought about* it, during the course of my recovery.

As usual, far wiser persons than I have discussed the issue at hand...

"WE APPRECIATE THIS!"

In their book *The Spirituality of Imperfection,* Ernest Kurtz and Katherine Ketcham offer a definition of the spiritual as "other-than-material." Methamphetamine and other drugs—my poor choices leading to my addiction—took away almost everything of a material nature. Thus, my addiction served a purpose, was a sort of twisted blessing. It forced me along a spiritual pathway, one I might otherwise never have undertaken.

"YOU HAD TO RELY UPON WHAT YOU COULD NOT SEE OR TOUCH."

A story about the Dalai Lama goes something like this: He is asked, "What is the best religion?" The questioner believes the answer will be Buddhism, because it is the oldest. But the Dalai Lama responds that the best religion is the one that makes the practitioner the best person. The most compassionate,

Nineteen: Families

grateful, loving, etc.

One Saturday night in April, many years into my recovery, I retire to bed early, only to awake soon afterwards with wrenching chest pain. A worst nightmare…I've long been concerned my drug abuse caused lasting damage to my heart, damage that would return to haunt me. Was this the haunting? The agony won't subside. Of all the times I thought I might OD on cocaine, meth, ecstasy, or whatever, I never once seriously considered calling 911. But now, I feel there's no choice. The chest pain is so great, I can barley speak after dialing the phone.

An ambulance ride and Emergency Room visit later, the diagnosis is…an esophageal issue! For weeks I'd been on a heavy cayenne pepper diet, attempting to regulate my calorie intake by spicing my food beyond edible. I even put cayenne pepper in my coffee.

"BUT…COFFEE HAS NO CALORIES!"

"A lot of people are fooled," the ER doctor, a young man wearing a clean hospital coat, explains. "Esophagus spasms feel like a heart attack. The esophagus is right behind the heart."

I sit up on the gurney as electrodes are removed from my torso.

"Maybe cut back on the cayenne," he advises me before signing my release papers.

As a light rain falls just after midnight, I wander the streets near the University of San Francisco in my pajamas, trying to catch a bus home. Bewildered, yet grateful.

The following Sunday morning finds me at Epic Church, where I've been attending gatherings for a couple months. From the stage, Pastor Ben Pilgreen delivers a message. He tells a story of the Apostle Peter addressing a crowd of several thousand. Many members of the audience appear to be drunk (Peter's audience, that is, not the audience at Epic). But those who hear Peter's words, regarding their error in judgement...

"AN *ERROR IN JUDGEMENT?* THEY NAILED GOD'S ONLY SON TO A WOODEN CROSS."

...understand the gravity of their situation. And they are cut to the heart.

Cut to the heart.

Pastor Ben's exact words, quoted from the Bible.

Ben explains that Peter's message inspired three thousand to be baptized that day. "We don't usually do this," Ben announces from the stage. "But today, here at Epic, anyone who wants to be baptized can come on up."

If my "heart attack" of the previous night, coupled with Ben's story of being *cut to the heart,* isn't some sort of sign...

I rise from my seat and make my way forward.

A few minutes later, Pastor Ben plunges me under, then brings me back up.

I join an Epic community. The Faith and Work Group meets Tuesdays, 7:30 in the morning. Made up of entrepreneurs and executives, leaders and searchers, the Faith and Work Group, like the larger Epic community—like Rhino Toastmasters and Defy Ventures—accepts and supports me. Through their compassion, and the compassion of many others, I become greater able to lead that *spiritual life.*

So, for me personally, it seems, Christianity is the best religion.

Which doesn't mean I feel any particular religion is the best for you. Or anyone else.

Nineteen: Families

The members of the Faith & Work Group, the leaders and members of Epic, are wonderful people...were they Hindu, Muslim, or Zen Buddhist, I'd still want to be a part of their community.

Someone once explained to me, being Christian means trying to be more like Christ...

"IN THE BIBLE, JESUS WAS A PRETTY DECENT GUY!"

He fed the hungry, healed the sick, showed the trodden-upon their path to faith. His words taught me not to be afraid of those who kill the body; they can do no more. When it comes to Bible stories, I try not to get caught up debating myself whether something must be historically accurate in order to be relevant to my life.

"SOMETHING DOESN'T NECESSARILY HAVE TO BE REAL IN ORDER TO TEACH LESSONS."

I continue to meditate every morning (most mornings, anyway). Conducting a personal search for spiritual meaning. As I understand Jesus did—as I understand the Buddha and the Prophet Muhammad did.

I hope my story might inspire you to find your own brand of other-than-material...to discover your own Rhino Toastmasters, Defy Ventures, FBI, or Epic Church. I hope what you find helps you surmount your own challenges. You may be facing down your own Boolean FBI, may be seeking answers to your own story of Omar. Your obstacles may well be greater than mine. During those very darkest times in my recovery...when fear of the Boolean FBI gripped me like a vise, when doubts about Omar crushed me like an avalanche...spirituality proved to be enough to get me through.

And whether or not you have any interest in spirituality, Omar, or the Boolean FBI, you can perhaps learn more about yourself by learning something of the mind of a schizophrenic.

Twenty:
Hands

Success is to be measured not so much by the position that one has reached in life as by the obstacles he or she has overcome.

—Booker T. Washington

In the 1960s, a woman named Mary Barnes received treatment for schizophrenia in Kingsley Hall, in England.

I read about her in *Them*, by Jon Ronson.

(Ronson also wrote *Men Who Stare at Goats,* about the military's experiments with telepathy and the paranormal.)

Mary Barnes received a special sort of therapy.

Her doctors allowed her to express herself freely.

Unfortunately, she discovered an unusual means of free self-expression…

She smeared the walls of her room with her own excrement.

Thus, a problem for her doctors.

On one hand, they felt self-expression to be vital to her recovery.

On the other hand, the smell emanating from her room overpowered the other patients, staff, and visitors.

They happened upon the solution when someone realized Barnes wasn't so much smearing her excrement…

As was she painting with it.

When they provided actual paint, she substituted it for her other medium.

Not only did doctors solve a troubling problem…

Mary Barnes went on to become a well-known artist.

Her paintings give viewers a glimpse into the mind of a schizophrenic.

In the 1960s, my current sponsor, Dean, still drank, used drugs.

I don't write much about Dean.

It's like trying to write about God.

If you meet Dean in person, you'll find my description only falls short.

There's an analogy of nurturing a human being as being like growing a plant. You ensure your plant has proper soil, water, sunshine. But you don't instruct your plant to "sprout your next leaf at this place on your stem" or "put forth a blossom at noon tomorrow."

Your plant grows on its own, given proper conditions.

Dean gives me those proper conditions.

In June 2018, a month after graduating the FBI Citizens Academy…

I start publishing an e-newsletter called *Meditations on Meth* and distribute it to about a hundred friends and supporters.

One issue I call "Hands."

"In order to achieve the life I wanted, I had been dealt, it seemed to me, the worst possible hand." —James Baldwin, "Letter from

Twenty: Hands

a Region in My Mind"

I read those words of Baldwin's the other day and realized...

I often believed the same applied to me.

Yet all the while, the truth was: I remained too mired in resentment—of the most selfish and self-centered varieties—to appreciate life had, in fact, dealt me a very good hand.

A hand I threw away to meth addiction.

One person who taught me the most about overcoming resentments is my AA sponsor...

I'll call him "Dean."

Dean had been involved in the civil rights movement and affiliated with the Black Panthers.

He'd visited the White House at the invitation of then-President Jimmy Carter.

Was a successful businessman, too.

But Dean fell prey to alcoholism...

And ended up switching careers to become, as he terms it, a 'petroleum transfer engineer.'

(He pumped gas)

When he began sponsoring me, Dean—in his seventies—was over twenty years sober, a competitive runner and cyclist.

He'd beaten prostate cancer, rebuilt his career (in finance, not pumping gas) and helped many, many people overcome alcoholism and addiction.

He had numerous options from which to choose, when it came to how to spend his time...

Why spend it with me? A whiny, overprivileged, resentment-filled guy who, even if he had cause to blame others for his problems, would only be doing so at the expense of taking responsibility to solve those problems.

Yet Dean took me to lunch after our sponsor meetings and introduced me to our server as his "brother from another mother."

He listened patiently to my complaints...

And painstakingly taught me things such as:

"Expectations are resentments under construction."

"Your ego is not your amigo."

Soon I found myself ending our conversations telling Dean I loved him.

(A spiritual love, not romantic)

Dean helped me learn how to replace resentments, with love.

I've read almost nothing of Baldwin's, and I've spent a lot of time with Dean…

Yet I know I have a lot to learn from both.

Thanks, Baldwin and Dean. I appreciate you and the many others like you, greater persons and thinkers than I…

For your efforts to pass along your wisdom…

Despite how little it seems I might've done to deserve it.

Dean, like Mary Barnes' doctors, understands…

If I'm allowed to express myself, eventually my excrement will turn to paint.

I can draw lines made of words.

(Instead of lines of meth)

I may never become the caliber of artist as Barnes.

Yet for a guy stuck so long at the business end of a meth pipe, behind the Spalding Grey Portcullis, and fixed in conspiracy theories…

These days, almost any kind of picture is worth framing.

Twenty: Hands

There was a time—and this is *years clean off meth*—I remained so wrapped up in the "conspiracy" around Omar, I'd decided to bring his story to light it by setting myself on fire on a downtown San Francisco sidewalk. After mailing details about Omar to all the major media outlets.

"THEY WOULD HAVE TO PAY ATTENTION TO US! WE WOULD BE ON FIRE, AFTER ALL."

Fortunately, others inspired me to stay cool.

To spend years banging away on the keyboard…

> Instead of a last few seconds engulfed in anger at myself, misdirected at others.
>
> Today, I believe in myself.
>
> I feel fulfilled and confident, that I'm making contributions to the world around me.
>
> A spirit of gratitude pulls me along…I don't stay stuck in the difficult times.

Yes, I'm grateful to Dean…

To Officer Pagano (she's Captain Pagano today), Sebastian, Joe Alioto, and the many others…

"DON'T FORGET US, YOUR SPOUSES!"

For teaching me how to turn my mind's excrement into love.

For taking a chance on me…for believing I deserved a second chance, even if I didn't believe it.

Yet I'm also grateful for the Oakmont bullies, Boolean Uncle Jupiter, and the Boolean FBI.

They taught me to keep getting up, to have courage.

They, and many others, gave me new forms of paint.

Made me believe it's possible I have something you might want to read about.

As to whether it's possible to turn a life completely around, conquer fears, and achieve a dream?

You have the answer in your hands.

CPSIA information can be obtained
at www.ICGtesting.com
Printed in the USA
JSHW032125121021
19529JS00005B/47